UNLOCKING YOUR DESTINY

UNLOCKING YOUR DESTINY

explore your inner world

LESSONS ON NUMEROLOGY, LO SHU GRID
LIFE-PATH, WEALTH, AND HAPPINESS

SANTU ROY

Contents

Prologue

How wonderful it would be if we were all given planet's and number's governing principles and rules the day we were born. It is imperative that we refrain from categorising planets and numbers as inherently 'bad' or 'negative,' and instead strive to understand the underlying significance of planetary influences those resonated with thousands of people.

Numerology principles and rules will free you to achieve a purposeful and no-limit life with abundance. It is critical to grasp the principles that the planet expects you to follow as a rules.

There are many people who use quick remedies for common diseases, but do not consider the spiritual potential of remedies for complicated, prolonged illnesses, career and relationship challenges.

We should embrace astrology, numerology, face reading as daily tools for a better life, just as we accept and adopt technological advances. We should strive to understand, use these sciences achieving our life's purpose and find happiness.

Numbers plays signified role in human history, from ancient times to the present day, and considered fundamental components of the universe.

Numerology is a study of hidden meanings, symbols, numbers, and letters. The study of the universe and the human mind via the application of values and meanings.

This book explores the captivating realm-of numerology, its practical application revealing insights into personality traits, strengths, weaknesses, and life path.

You gain a deeper understanding of yourselves, the world, and explore numbers while choosing a career path, understanding your surroundings and workplace.

"I believe, life is a never-ending cycle that returns to the beginning. My journey is to uncover my true purpose. Although wealth is desirable, I aspire to attain perfect health, develop my intellect, and elevate my spiritual nature. Though we appear equal in dignity, our fates, purposes, and truths differ from one another. I was uncertain until numerology revealed my destiny. Soon I decoded a life-book, a map, and my destiny became clear."

Disclaimer

"I believed and have benefited from numerology, which inspired me to write this book. However, the information presented is for educational and entertainment purposes only. The numerology study deals with the symbolism and numbers, providing insights into a person's life and future. This book is not meant to diagnose, treat, cure, or prevent any medical or financial condition.

The interpretations presented are not prescriptive or critical, but aim to highlight the humanitarian potential of numerology faiths. It is important to use personal judgment, consult with professionals for any questions or concerns. The practice of numerology may not be accepted by all individuals or belief systems. By reading this book, the reader acknowledges their responsibility, actions taken based on the information provided as the author and publisher disclaim liability or responsibility for any loss or damage resulting from its use."

Acknowledgements

I must state: Nothing equates good Karma.

Writing a book is never a solo effort, and this numerology book is no exception. I would like to express my gratitude to the following individuals who have contributed to the creation of this book:

First and foremost, I would like to thank my family for their unwavering support and encouragement throughout this project. Your love, understanding have been my guiding light, and I am truly grateful for all that you have done.

I would also like to thank my friends, good wishers, relatives and colleagues who have provided me with valuable feedback, insights, and encouragement throughout the writing process. Your support has been invaluable, and I am blessed to have you in my life.

I am grateful to the numerology teachers, research documents, books and practitioners who have generously shared their knowledge and expertise with me over the years. Your teachings have been an inspiration and have helped me deepen my understanding of this ancient practice.

I would like to acknowledge the many authors, researchers, scholars whose work has informed and influenced my writing. Your contributions to the field of numerology are immeasurable, and I am honoured to be a part of this community.

I am grateful to the publisher, editors, and production team who have worked tirelessly to bring this book to life. Your professionalism, dedication, and attention to detail have made this a truly collaborative effort.

Lastly, I want to express my gratitude to the readers who will pick up this book and embark on their own numerology journey. It is my hope that this book will inspire and empower you to discover the hidden meanings and potentials within your own life.

Thank you all for your support and for being a part of this journey with me.

Sincerely,

Santu Roy

Preface

This numerology book provides a guide to understanding numbers. It covers the history, origins, methods, and how to calculate important numbers of those drives you.

The book includes descriptions of each number and exercises to help you apply this knowledge to your own existence. It offers guidance on how to use numerology to enhance personal, professional relationships, and how to navigate life's challenges and opportunities.

I have studied numbers practices from East and West, including Pythagorean, Chaldean, Vedic, and Chinese numerology, thanks to my journey leading me to incredible teachers and books.

I offer my prayers to the Nava Grahas, Lord Ganesha, and I am excited to introduce my second book, "Unlocking Your Destiny," following last year's "The Power of Self Brainwash." I hope that this work encourages, bolsters you to discover the concealed implications and capabilities of your own life, no matter if you are a novice or an expert practitioner.

Chapter 1

Human Aura and Energy

Have you ever heard of the aura? It's an amazing electromagnetic field that surrounds and interpenetrates your physical body, and it reflects your emotional and spiritual states! Your energy field, or life force, flows through your body and helps keep good health and vitality. But here's the thing: if your aura is out of balance, it can affect your health, well-being, and relationships.

That's where numerology comes in - it helps you achieve a harmonious aura and balance your energy! By aligning with the nature laws and establishing a protective, preventive shield through your aura, you live a fulfilled, purposeful, and happier life. Give numerology a chance and see what it does for you.

In numerology, we calculate a person's life-path and destiny number. Further, we utilise this information to get an insight into strengths, weaknesses, and potential. Everything in the universe vibrates certain energy which affects our life. Aura balancing restores a harmony around the body. Imbalances in the aura leads to physical, emotional, and spiritual problems.

Meditation, energy healing and numerology restores a balanced aura and promote well-being. The decision to believe in the power of numerology and aura balancing is a personal choice. However, many reported positive experiences and helped others achieve greater balance and harmony in their lives. You appear harmonious with the nature; you learn to keep a balanced life mentally, emotionally, and physically, bringing you the best of everything in life for:

- Making a well-thought decision

- Making a purposeful life

- Reducing your baggage and loving yourself

- Enhancing your potential

- Maintaining a good health and bring more wealth

- Defend against infections and illness

- Overcome difficulties

- Maintain healthy relationships

- Bringing true love

Chapter 2

Introduction

You wish, desire to stay healthy, wealthy, known and want to achieve a success? Do you want to change your perspective on life and live happier with pleasure?

- Knowing your personality and destiny number is important

- Enhancing the quality of your life is crucial

- Making wise judgments leads to better career choices

- Managing daily difficulties is vital

- Understanding your soul's desires is significant

- Learning to understand people around you is important

- Evaluating if a specific relationship is rewarding is crucial

- Defining business and relationship odds is essential.

Learn to say what you really want in life and know the truth about your heart's desire.

Have you considered using numerology as a tool for personal guidance? You would learn how to live a fulfilling life by digging into this ancient discipline, discovering your innate powers and true potential. This will allow you to interact with the world and discover facets of your personality.

We have used numerology for centuries to help ourselves and our place in the world through the fundamental of vibration.

Everything in the universe vibrates energy, hence numerology guides us to get a better grasp of ourselves and our relationship with the cosmos.

Pythagorean, Kabbalah, Chinese, Vedic, and Chaldean are a few numerology systems. Numerology determines the meanings of the numbers 1 through 9.

Chaldean numerology is a 4,000-year-old system that began in Babylon. Which gives each English letter a numerical value. In contrast to the Pythagorean system,

Chaldean numerology does not assign letters a numerical value to the number 9.

Numerology is easier to understand than other fields within the spiritually relevant studies of Astrology, Taro Cards, Palmistry, Vastu, Face Reading, and Graphology.

When numbers are out of sync, problems arise. Each digit in numerology represents a planet, influential tone, and colour. A name contains information regarding one's fate and the experiences along their life path.

One of the unique aspect of Chaldean numerology is the use of its compound numbers, which are formed by combining two or more digits. These compound numbers have their own unique symbolism, meaning, and provide insight into a person's personality.

Each alphabet correlates a number and is used to analyse a name using numbers. The 26 letters are used to translate every poetry, novel, love letter, business letter, expression of romance and emotion.

Chaldean numerology is a powerful tool for self-discovery and personal growth. By understanding the symbolism, energy of numbers, we gain insight into ourselves, our relationships, and our life path.

Whether you are a novice or a seasoned practitioner, Chaldean numerology offers a fascinating, a system for exploring the hidden meanings and potentials within our lives.

Chapter 3

Chaldean Numerology

Chaldean numerology originated in Babylonia is the oldest decoding method. The Chaldeans recognised energy in everything, linked sound, vibration, and numbers to letters.

Your name holds energy, and vibrations reveal a lot about your attitudes, traits, and power level. There are numbers all across the world, and you are just as affected as everyone else.

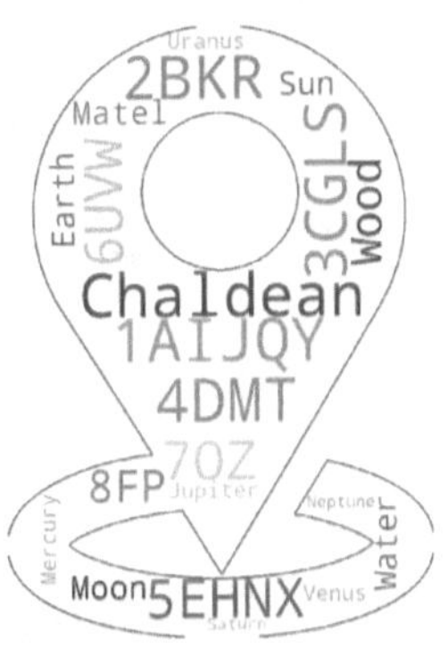

Based on Vedic/Indian numerology, they considered Chaldean system as the origin of numerology. Each number from one (1) to nine (9) governed a planet and associated with a group of alphabet for name numerology.

They assigned letters between number 1 to 8 for name numerology calculation. But there is no alphabet allocated to number 9 in the Chaldean system. They believed the number 9 a sacred number when added to other numbers do not change the value.

It's vital to note that word vibration is being applied in place of letters for name numerology. As a result, how you write your name is not signifies as how it pronounce. The Chaldean practice does not analyse a person's characteristics with one number, rather stressed on considering compound numbers.

The majority of numerologists believe in the concept of master numbers. They assert that the master numbers eleven (11) and twenty-two (22) are as complicated compared to single digit.

The time has come for me to fulfil unspoken agreement originated from the universe itself: to share my knowledge of Chaldean numerology with you through this book. As I enjoyed being a part of its creation, I hope you appreciate the result as much as I did.

As you read through the book, you would explore learning to calculate the hidden meaning of your "Name", "Birth number", "Life path number", "Destiny number". You would gain insights throughout the book as it continues to decode, guide, and explain each pillar of your life. With a positive state of mind, it is easier to generate ideas, align yourself to the progressive pathway, bringing wealth, success, and bliss.

"If you want to find the secrets of the universe, think in terms of energy, frequency, and vibration."

Nikola Tesla

The quote would make you stay motivated reading this book bringing you the best possible accuracy in decoding yourself and others as you share your knowledge learned from reading this book. Practice leads to experience, experience leads to knowledge, and generates the ability to perform well.

Having faith in numerology is important for spiritual growth and doing something different for others. Commit to learn nitty-gritty from this book, be ready to take up new reading within your known people, and you would be alright being comfortable to decode each name, letters, birth date related to everything about anyone you apply these concepts, and help others in their way of life.

Chapter 4

Benefits of Numerology

The numerology is a great tool that helps you discover your birthday, and which life-path you should follow. Once you find a best suitable life's purpose, you continue a happy life connecting with others, managing relationships, and attracting compatible people into your life.

They generate harmony and guides you through:

Self-discovery: Numerology be a powerful tool for self-discovery and self-awareness. By analysing a numerological chart, you gain insights into your personality, strengths, weaknesses, and life purpose.

Relationship compatibility: By analysing the numerological charts of two individuals, a numerologist determines whether they are likely to be compatible and successful in a romantic or business relationship.

Career guidance: Numerology provides guidance on career paths, help individuals to identify their strengths and weaknesses in relation to their chosen career.

Personal growth: Use numerology as a tool for personal growth and self-improvement. By identifying areas of weakness in your numerological chart, you could focus on improving those areas and developing your strengths.

Decision-making: Numerology could provide guidance and insight when making important life decisions. By analysing the numerological implications of a particular decision, you make informed choices that are aligned with your life path and overall well-being.

Benefits of numerology are many and helps individuals to gain a deeper understanding of themselves and their place in the world. It is important to work with a reputable numerologist or expert in this field to ensure that the interpretations, guidance provided are accurate and meaningful.

Chapter 5

Numbers

Numbers are present in all places as they have been a part of your life since the day you were born in the universe. One of the most important aspects of mastering numerology is understanding each numeral and its associated meaning from 1 to 9.

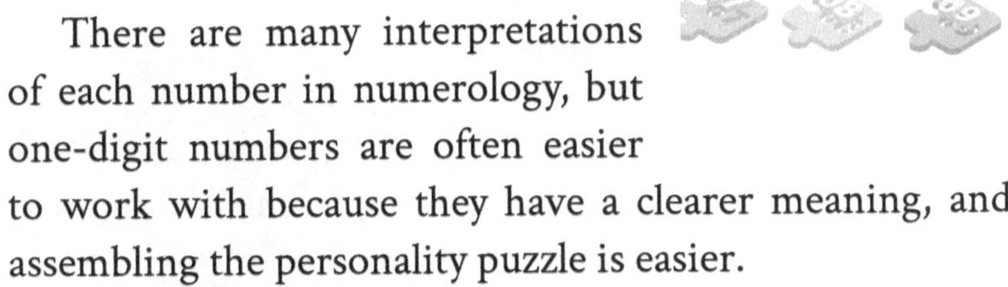

Even: 2, 4, 6, 8 Odd: 1, 3, 5, 7, 9.

There are many interpretations of each number in numerology, but one-digit numbers are often easier to work with because they have a clearer meaning, and assembling the personality puzzle is easier.

In this chapter, you would understand the basic quality of each number 1 through 9, 11 and 22 (the master numbers). Every name and identity equates a digit and explains its meaning, discussed in the later chapters in this book.

Zero (0)

The concept of Zero, also known as Shoonya or the Void in the East, holds no value on its own as it is an abstract concept, unlike concrete numbers. However, its introduction has significantly contributed to the fields of mathematics, science, and modern technology. Although we do not typically consider zero a number as it holds no quantity or purpose, it represents rebirth, renewal, infinity, and everything and nothing all at once. Its inclusion in mathematical analysis has become necessary and undeniable due to its importance.

Zero is often seen as a starting point for fresh possibilities, and although it may represent nothingness, its addition to other numbers results in exponential growth (e.g. 10, 1000, 10000). The applications of zero are limitless, but it often focuses on the growth or decrease of matter, demonstrating attributes such as intensity, power, and creation, while also taking and giving.

One (1)

1 is the base of the other numbers, a leader who stands straight and confident. To meet success, those individuals are clear-headed, creative, and have a winning mind.

A person represented by the number 1 dislikes authorities because he or she strives to become an authority themselves. Because there is no one else to support them, they bound by their innate ego and impulses.

Courage, aspiration, goal-oriented thinking, proactivity, self-confidence drive the pursuit of experiences and successes.

1 stands by itself like a lamppost that is self-reliant, dominant and holds leadership qualities. Those born on 1st, 10th, 19th and 28th of any month experience the influence of planet Sun's energy, vibration and strength.

The planet Sun governs the number 1 and represents activity. It has knowledge of what will happen, as well as the guts, boldness, determination, and wisdom to move in a location where everything is blank and empty.

Positive Qualities

- Resourcefulness

- Individuality

- Leadership through innovation

- Self-assurance

- Strong beliefs

Negative Traits

- Selfishness

- Introverts

- Aggression

- Dominance

- Impulsiveness

Two (2)

Considering number one (1) as an independent man, we would consider number two (two) as a woman, since this number is easier to understand. Pairs, duality, adaptability, wholeness, flexibility, and harmony are characteristics of the number 2.

The planet Moon rules the 2.

Those born on the 2nd, 11th, 20th, and 29th enjoy all the qualities of this planet.
Those with this energy exhibit a balance of romanticism and domesticity. These individuals display qualities of tenderness, benevolence, and an absence of aggressive or dominant behaviour. They possess a unique ability to comprehend and appreciate both perspectives of an issue, enabling them to tackle problems from a well-rounded and impartial standpoint.

Their intuition serves them well in managing differences, disagreements, and obstacles, enabling them to remain calm and level-headed in difficult situations.

Positive Qualities

- Duality
- Facilitator
- Diplomacy
- Integrity
- Spiritual

Negative Traits

- Predominant mind
- Indifferent
- Careless
- Unsociable
- Unable to make up his/her mind

Three (3)

In numerology, the number 3 holds significant importance as it is the first digit in the Heavenly Triad, which comprises the numbers 3, 6, and 9. Jupiter governs those born on the 3rd, 12th, 21st, and 30th of the month. Its integrity brings in imagination, procreation, motion, thought, a certain amount of luck and magic.

Individuals with the number 3 have a strong desire to accomplish their goals, they are child like, master of material achievement through creative ability and expression. Those born with a birthday number of 3 are typically known for their creativity, enthusiasm, quick-wittedness, sense of humour, and ability to uplift those around them.

Because of Jupiter's association with the number three, this energy assists young people in their education, growth, and career goals. They have a natural ability to express themselves and may excel in fields such as art, music, writing, or acting. We believe that the number 3 is growth, expansion, making it a favourable number in business and personal growth.

Positive Qualities

- Curiosity and joyous

- Self-expression

- Empathetic

- Creative communication

- Consciousness, and positivity

- Satisfaction

Negative Traits

- Obsessions

- Selfish

- Sensual

- Unresponsive

- Lack of motivation

Four (4)

In numerology, we perceive the number 4 as the shadow number of the number 1. The number 4 represents management, regularity, and practicality. We consider those who are born on 4th, 13th, 22nd and 31st of the month as four.

A person with a birthday number of 4 stays practical, reliable, hard-working, honest and known for their self-discipline.

Understanding them takes time as they appear intense, fearful, worry and confused.

Further, the number four (4) defined as repetitive stability, hard-working, scheduled work, productivity, wellbeing, regulations, technique, dependability, and strength.

Hence, the 4 want to revolutionise with new ideas, but most people hate new ideas because they take them outside their comfort zones.

Positive Qualities

- Attention and consistency

- Rationality

- Realism

- Sincerity

- Persistence, and foundation

Negative Traits

- Unplanned, lack of imagination

- Excessive seriousness

- Tremendous detail

- Stubbornness

- Fixed viewpoints, misunderstanding

Five (5)

The planet Mercury influences people born on 5th, 14th, and 23rd of the month. The number Five (5) sits at the centre of 1 to 10, it shows the balanced symbol, administration, and control over the condition.

People represented by the number 5 are natural speakers. They have great social skills and they get along with everyone. Those with number 5 described as adventurous and thrive for environments that are constantly changing.

We consider 5 a balanced number, as it occupies the middle ground between extremes.

Charm, relationships, and the capacity to communicate are attributes shared by the numbers 5 and 3. As a result, we regard people with a 5 personality as pleasing. There is a connection between the number 5 and freedom and versatility. The number 5 has an affinity for curious mind.

Positive Qualities

- Action oriented

- Administration

- Promoting ideas

- Freedom loving

- Quickness, and curiosity

Negative Traits

- Anxiousness

- Unhappiness

- Mood Swing

- Sharp Speech

- Temper, dissatisfaction, impatience

Six (6)

The number 6 is the second number in the trinity 3, 6, and 9. Those born on 6th, 15th, or 24th of the month bear the quality of number 6 under the planet Venus. A birthday number 6 is someone who prefers a strong family bonding.

Individuals born with a birthday number 6 typically value strong family bonds and connections. They possess artistic and idealistic qualities and have a natural inclination towards nurturing and comforting others.

These individuals often prioritise the well-being and happiness of their loved ones and go to great lengths to create a harmonious and supportive environment for those around them..

It is the vibration of a home seeker, returning home, flying back to the nest, seeking shelter from the storm. It is the vibration of warmth and security.

The 6 energy is associated with love for children, animals, and music.

Positive Qualities

- Artistic
- Visionary, humanist
- Truth, and righteousness
- Family values, family loving
- Conventional, and welfare

Negative Traits

- Compassionate
- Commitment
- Obscenity, and outspokenness
- Timidity, and slowness in decision-making
- Stubbornness
- Complaint, egoistic

Seven (7)

The number 7 symbolises insight, the search for deeper meaning in things, and those represents the number 7 have many deep thoughts in their mind. The number 7 governs those born on the 7th, 16th, and 25th of the month, while Neptune is the rolling planet for number 7 in west, but in Vedic system its Ketu.

They characterise a person with a birthday number of 7 as analytical, a decision making and private care giver.

The number 7 own intelligence, logical ideas, and a analysing brain. This number brings in mystical questions and why there are 7 colours of the rainbow, 7 chakra, 7 days in a week and 7 notes on the scale of a piano.

A direct and varied life experience coupled with deep, intellectual aim, and spiritual thought is the only way to reach number 7. We must acknowledge its potential, honour it, respect it and utilise it. The number is protected to prevent it from being seen or understood.

Positive Qualities

- Technology, and science

- Analytical abilities

- Exploration

- Computation

- Occultist, dignity, and perfectionist

- Manner, and personality

Negative Traits

- Sentimental intelligence

- Isolation, and resentment

- Reserve, and skepticism

- Disproportionate, and over-analysis

- Temper, and individualism, critical views

Eight (8)

For those whose birthday falls on 8th, 17th, and 26th of the month, we consider their number to be eight (8) and the planet Saturn governs this number.

Number 8 individuals have natural talents for financial management and overseeing large projects with ambition and authority. They value discipline and keep a consistent lifestyle, even in the face of the inevitable difficulties that come with life.

They are driven by a desire to succeed and able to manage challenges.

Eight (8) focuses on balancing between the material and spiritual world.

When it is a source of power and strength, the number 8 is also refer money. Research and study of individuals with this number in their chart or life path with leads to wealth or power. Wealthy individuals are more likely to have the number 8.

Positive Qualities

- Responsibility

- Attention to detail

- Efficiency and supervision

- Execution ability, and operational performance

- Awareness, judgement, and organisation

Negative Traits

- Tiredness

- Unable to focus

- Overreaction, and tension

- Repressing others

- Demanding, and commanding

Nine (9)

The number 9 is the last number in the trinity of 3, 6 and 9. We consider it a divine number as it is associated with selflessness, compassion, and humanitarianism. People who are influenced by this number are said to have a deep understanding of human nature and a strong desire to help others. They believed to possess a strong intuition and a deep connection to the universe.

However, the number 9 is also associated with endings and closures. It signifies the completion of a cycle, and the need to let go of the old in order to make room for the new.

The planet Mars governs number nine (9) and those born on the 9th, 18th or 27th influenced through this number's energy. They are determined to succeed. These people are considerate, open-minded, and diligent. They could be either the administrator or commander-in-chief.

Positive Traits

- Love, perfection and taking action
- Ideality, and compassion
- Humanitarianism, and philanthropy
- Forgiveness, and leaders in charitable activity
- Artistic, writers, and musicians

Negative Traits

- Too much aggression
- Self-centredness
- Impulsiveness, and possessiveness
- Demanding, and mood swings
- Inability to use talents
- Carelessness

Eleven (11)

11/2, and 22/4 are master numbers. A master number is a double-digit-number repeats itself and comes from a single root number. The number 11 is a master number with 1 repeated and the reduced number is 2 (1 + 1 = 2) a root number.

The number 11/2 referred as the spiritual messenger, as they show deep commitment to bringing spiritual messages to Earth. An 11/2's we perceive good energy as motivating and uplifting, as well as intuitive, sensitive, and too exuberant.

The numerology master number 11/2 symbolises the interplay between masculine and feminine, active and receptive energies, signifying that two individuals traverse the space to achieve balance. The two pillars of a gateway represent this compound number, with the centre point between them signifying a choice towards a positive, upward path. Success will follow if one is on the correct path.

Positive Qualities

- Inspirational
- Intuitive
- Intellectual
- Innovative and Creative
- Co-operative

Negative Traits

- Egocentric
- Depressive
- Overly sensitive
- Susceptible to stress

Twenty -Two (22)

People have labeled the number twenty-two (22/4) as the master builder. 22/4 people, are a planner, builder and a visionary who could see "big picture" through smaller details.

They may work as musicians, composers, interpreters, instructors, ministers, painters, and decorators, among other professions. They love to share, encourage, and uplift other people.

Those with 22/4 know how to combine inspirational ideas with physique, and they bring the ability to show.

Yet 22 is less effective than the 11, indeed adaptable to the earth's plane; it manifest material success since its root is 4.

You could see a 22/4 as the force behind great undertakings as they are deft organisers and ambitious workers. Other higher vibrations associated with the 22/4 are idealism, intuition, confidence and wisdom.

Positive Qualities

- Revolutionary

- Ambitious

- Intelligent

- Realistic

- bursting with potential

Negative Traits

- Egocentric

- Depressive

- Overly sensitive

- Susceptible to stress

- Emotionally controlled

- Insensitive

Chapter 6

Planets

Numerology gives importance to the Navagrahas, or the nine planets, as they shape our lives and fate. Every planet has its own unique energy and influence, which have a profound effect on our personality traits, relationships, and paths in life.

Besides nine planets, Vedic numerology includes the signified influence of Rahu and Ketu, the two shadow planets, in shaping our lives and destiny.

The Sun (Surya) represents our individuality, ego, and self-expression. It holds immense power and is associated with leadership, creativity, and vitality.

The Moon (Chandra) symbolises our emotions, intuition, and subconscious mind. It is related to nurturing, sensitivity, and creativity.

Mars (Mangal) represents our passion, energy, and ambition. It is associated with courage, aggression, and determination.

Mercury (Budha): The planet Mercury mirrors our communication skills, intellect, and analytical abilities. It is associated with adaptability, versatility, and mental agility.

Jupiter (Guru): Jupiter is our wisdom, knowledge, and spirituality. It is associated with growth, abundance, and expansion.

Venus (Shukra): The planet Venus shows our love, relationships, and creativity. It is associated with beauty, harmony, and sensuality.

Saturn (Shani): Saturn is our discipline, responsibility, and hard work. It is associated with challenges, obstacles, and lessons.

Rahu: Rahu is a shadow planet that is our desires and ambitions. It is associated with materialism, obsession, and illusion.

Ketu: Ketu is another shadow planet that describes our spirituality and detachment. It is associated with detachment, liberation, and enlightenment.

Depending on an individual's birth chart and life path, each planet has its own unique energy and influence. It is possible to gain insight into our strengths, challenges, and life purpose when we understand the signifies and symbolism of each planet.

The Sun is the King; the Moon is the Queen, Mars is the Commander-in-Chief, Mercury is the Prince, Jupiter is the Minister of Religion, Venus is the Minister of Politics, and Saturn is the Lord of Justice.

Planets, numbers, and alphabet stay linked, and emit vibrations, which aid in drawing pseudo-scientific inferences from words, names, and concepts.

In the Hindu system, the number 4 corresponds to Rahu (the Moon's north node), but in the Western system, it is associated with the Sun and Uranus. In the Hindu system, the number 7 belongs to Ketu (the Moon's south node), whereas in the Western system, it is associated with the Moon and Neptune.

Each number and associated English alphabet carry energy from the planet to which we assign them, as we allot a number to the above 9 planets.

The planets and numbers in numerology emit a unique vibration that aids individuals in determining their life path. To comprehend an individual's personality traits and how others perceive them, a definitive reading is required to understand the planet's impact on their life.

Although   not an exact science, numerology relies on logical procedures and relational interpretations based on information on the planetary bodies found in the scriptures.

Numerology associates each number with a specific planet and day, depending on the vibrational energy and symbolism of each number and planet, as well as their corresponding letters in the alphabet. In Jyotish and astrology study, the nine planets (navagrahas) used are the luminaries (the Sun and Moon) and the grahas (Mercury, Venus, Mars, Jupiter, Saturn, Rahu, and Ketu).

Each planet and its corresponding number have their own symbolism and energy in numerology. For instance, in the family tree, the SUN is the father, MOON is the mother, MARS represents the brother, MERCURY is the uncle, JUPITER represents the children, VENUS is the wife, SATURN represents the self, RAHU is the grandfather, and KETU is the grandmother. These associations reveal different aspects of a person's personality and life path.

Numbers and week-days

- Sunday: 1 - 4

- Monday: 2 - 7

- Tuesday: 9

- Wednesday: 5

- Thursday: 3

- Friday: 6

- Saturday: 8

Numbers and Planets

- Sun: 1

- Moon: 2

- Jupiter: 3

- Rahu / Uranus: 4

- Mercury: 5

- Venus: 6

- Ketu / Neptune: 7

- Saturn: 8

- Mars: 9

THE SUN (1)

The Sun (Celestial King), the Solar system's father, is the hottest planet among others. It has the most signified influence on individual's personality.

It symbolise energy, father, consciousness, self-awareness, authority, reputation, and strength. It also relates to the motel gold and copper. 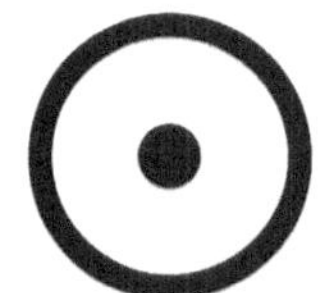

In numerology, the number One (1), is the planet Sun, and in astrology sign LEO.

We consider those born on 1st, 10th, 19th, 28th of any month as number-one (1), and they carry both good and bad side of the planet's quality. They seem clean, bad-tempered, and intelligent.

The number 1 is associated with an authoritative personality, likes freedom, is intelligent, and values life's luxuries. They excel as government personnel, ministers, and recipients of royal patronage.

The positive view of the Sun's influence is leadership; the negative is arrogance and intolerance.

THE MOON (2)

The Moon (the Celestial Queen), represents a person's "Mind," we regard it as a vital planet. It is the way we respond in life to the "mother" of the solar structure. With its female qualities, the Moon controls the moods and emotional responses to life conditions.

We relate the Moon to water because of its influence on tides. It displays changes, motions, and rhythms, as well as physical changes in life. The Moon is in charge of intuition, affection, and spirituality. The number-two (2) shows the planet Moon, and in astrology sign Cancer. Those influenced through this number, and the planet carries the Moon's energy. They are peaceful, sensitive, gentle, supportive, emphatic, emotional, fluctuating, well looking, perceptive, and pleasant. Those born on 2nd, 11th, 20th, 29th of any month do link to the planet Moon. They appear favourable, with pleasant conversation, yet are fickle and insatiable. The positive view of the Moon signifies balance, motherly approach, and fortunes; the negative aspects are moodiness, impulsiveness, and extreme inactivity.

THE JUPITER (3)

As the largest planet, Jupiter (the Celestial Minister) is known as the "Gurus" or "Teachers," an important planet for education. Symbolising improvement, expansion, and open-mindedness. It denotes moral, religious and philosophical beliefs, foreign, external affairs, and stands for virtues and justice, respect, and courage. Jupiter governs energy, ambition, and discipline.

The number-three (3), represents the planet Jupiter, and those influenced through this number, planet carries the Jupiter's energy. These people are courageous, healthy, energetic, and strong. They are rational, ambitious, spiritual, scholarly, enlightened, and disciplined.

We consider those born on 3rd, 12th, 21st, and 30th of any month to be number three (3) and they carry both good and rough side of the planet's quality. They have a large body, are tall, cheerful, and knowledgeable in many areas. Jupiter is pleasant, generous, and materialistic. Yet, Jupiter's wrong tendencies include hubris, exaggeration, and even vital work. It influences the liver and pituitary gland besides managing the body's repair.

THE RAHU (4)

Number 4 represents the planet Rahu. We could refer Rahu to Uranus. It just has the Demon's Head. The "Worldly Fame" always intrigues Rahu. They always draw it to materialistic goods. People reference the planet Rahu (Uranus) about its orientation when discussing the mysteries of the universe's formation.

Uranus in the chart represents how our need for independence and freedom manifests itself. It denotes the motivations underlying our hopes, wants, goals, and those imagined by the mind.

Number 4 persons are those born on the 4th, 13th, 22nd, and 31st of any month. These people are rebellious, unpredictable, obstinate, aggressive, moody, short-tempered, secretive, and impulsive.

Saturday, Sunday, and Monday are more fortunate or "lucky" for them, especially if their "own number" falls on one of these days, such as the 4th, 13th, 22nd, or 31st.

THE MERCURY (5)

The Mercury, the Budh in Hindi, (the Prince planet), the smallest planet functions as the messenger of the God, and describes a person's logical or communicative abilities.

"Mercury is the ruler of the cognitive process, and it discloses the psychological patterns and perceptions that affect the ability to make judgements, decision making and expressing ideas."

This planet is green, which represents balance, harmony, and hope. It soothe stressed nerves and the mind. As a result, this colour is beneficial to persons who have cardiac difficulties.

People born on 5th, 14th, 23th of any month do carry both good and bad qualities of this planet. They are good at communication, stay childish, bright, volatile, adaptable, free-spirited, progressive, rational, playful, princely, astute, sensitive, and bright. Mercury controls the nervous system, brain, lungs, and thyroid, it governs childhood and education. They could appear irrational, moody, fearlessness, and straightforwardness.

THE VENUS (6)

The Venus, Shukra in Hindi, (the beauty planet), is the planet which everyone seeks for and it acts as a "Princess" in the Celestial Cabinet. Venus shows Love, Romance, elegance and any relations in one's life.

The number Six (6) represents the planet Venus. It enhances Romanism, makes someone slow, sensual, sweet spoken, diplomatic and manipulative. People born on 6th, 15th, 24th of any month does influenced by this number and planet's both good and bad energy.

Six Rules wealth, sensuousness, and linked to music, automobiles, and sports. They are artistic, sensual, passionate, soft-spoken, gentle, innovative, and friendly.

Moon is pale white but Venus is bright white. The effects of the white colour are the same as in the Moon but Moon represents simplicity, while Venus represents sophistication. Venus is associated with friendship and love, the relationship with wild sexual passion is exaggerated. Venu controls throat, kidneys, and parathyroid glands.

THE KETU (7)

The Ketu is not a planet, but known as the Moon's South Node, Chhaya Grah OR shadow planet. It is uninterested in worldly fame and wants. It is opposite Rahu. This is a planet that seeks enlightenment. This shadow planet is brown in hue. Brown is not the primary colour in the spectrum. In eastern numerology, the number Seven (7), represents the planet Ketu, but in the West it denotes the planet Neptune. People born on the 7th, 16th, or 25th of any month are autonomous, original, and have a strong sense of identity. They are restless by nature and enjoy change and travel. They are impulsive, disruptive, social, artistic, intuitive, mystical, religious, insightful, dreamy, and nature-loving.

Those influenced by this planet appear intuitive and imaginative. It overrules spine, nervous systems, and the thalamus. The fortunate days are Sunday and Monday, especially if their "own number" or their interchangeable numbers of 1, 2, 4, such as the 1st, 2nd, 4th, 10th, 11th, 13th, 19th, 20th, 22nd, 28th, 29th, or 31st, fall on one of these days.

THE SATURN (8)

The Saturn, the Shani in Hindi, (The planet of judgement), symbolises the public. The planet is renowned for its wisdom. It judges you based on your Karma from your current birth and assigns you grade. It's a slow planet that takes time to produce results.

Saturn's rings are the extensive in the Solar System. Saturn's colour is black. Black is a relaxing hue for people who are upset, and we known it for its defensive powers. The number Eight (8), represents the planet Saturn, and those born on 8th, 17th, 26th of any month influenced through both positive and negative aspects. They carry their responsibilities and are capable enough to achieve the work done. The planet might bring difficulties, challenging situation for the individual to test the ability so one's stays hopeful, honest and persistence to receive the reward. They stay introverted, lonely, thoughtful, strong-willed, compassionate, repressive, and protective. The planet Saturn ruled the skin, bones, and teeth.

THE MARS (9)

The Mars, Mangal in Hindi, (Commander-in-chief), it shows our fighting prowess and ferocity. We are confident in facing any scenario. It is always in a state of "Hurry" and ready to fight. It shows the "rapid react" or "activeness" of a person. Mars's red hue emits somewhat yellowish rays. The distinction between Sun red and Mars red is that the red in the Sun represents monarchy, but the red in Mars represents violence.

The number Nine (9) represents the planet Mars, and those born on the 9th, 18th, and 27th of the month, carries both negative and positive qualities of the planet. They appear active, healthy, egoistic, restless, short-tempered, aggressive, warlike, strong, harsh, fighting, strong leadership, hard on the outside yet soft on the inside. Their other characteristics include fearlessness, tenacity, and dour. Mars protects the sex glands, urinary system, blood, and kidneys. They discovered that great enemies, injuries, and strain were caused when they noticed the number 9 to be more prevalent than usual in the dates and events of their lives.

Chapter 7

Day of Month

The following is a summary of the energies and characteristics associated with individuals born on specific days of the month:

1: Individuals born on the 1st of the month possess pure Sun energy and tend to be independent, self-motivated, assertive, and natural leaders.

2: Individuals born on the 2nd of the month possess pure Moon energy and tend to be sensitive, cooperative, diplomatic, and intuitive.

3: Individuals born on the 3rd of the month possess pure Jupiter energy and tend to be creative, expressive, optimistic, and social.

4: Individuals born on the 4th of the month possess pure Rahu/Uranus energy and tend to be practical, disciplined, hardworking, and reliable.

5: Individuals born on the 5th of the month possess pure Mercury energy and tend to be adventurous, versatile, freedom-loving, and curious.

6: Individuals born on the 6th of the month possess pure Venus energy and tend to be nurturing, responsible, compassionate, and family-oriented.

7: Individuals born on the 7th of the month possess pure Ketu/Neptune energy and tend to be analytical, intellectual, introspective, and spiritual.

8: Individuals born on the 8th of the month possess pure Saturn energy and tend to be ambitious, driven, authoritative, and powerful.

9: Individuals born on the 9th of the month possess pure Mars energy and tend to be humanitarian, compassionate, selfless, and idealistic.

10: Individuals born on the 10th of the month are symbolised by the "Wheel of Fortune" and possess characteristics of honor, faith, and self-confidence. As the 1's energy depletes due to the presence of 0, those born on this day exhibit reduced Sun energy. They are known to be resourceful, determined, confident, and independent.

11: Individuals born on the 11th of the month may experience a somewhat negative influence of the Sun's energy, amplified by the repeated 1, but they also receive the support of the Moon's energy, as 11 is reduced to 2. As a result, they tend to exhibit intuitive, spiritual, visionary, and sensitive qualities. However, they may also face great difficulties in their life journey.

12: Individuals born on the 12th of the month receive a mixed outcome of the energies of 1, 2, and 3, with 1 dominating 2. The symbolism associated with this number includes suffering and anxiety of the mind. It is also indicated as "the Sacrifice" or "the Victim," which may foreshadow a tendency to be sacrificed for the plans or intrigues of others. Despite this, individuals born on this day tend to exhibit adaptable, versatile, sociable, and expressive qualities.

13: Individuals born on the 13th of the month receive a mixed outcome of energies from the numbers 1, 3, and 4, with 1 being dominant while 3's energy depletes. In some ancient writings, it is said that those who understand the number 13 will be given power. Individuals born on this day tend to experience transformative, upheaval, regeneration, and change throughout their lives.

14: Individuals born on the 14th of the month receive a mixed outcome of energies from the numbers 1, 4, and 5, with 1 being dominant while 4's energy depletes. These individuals tend to be adventurous, courageous, adaptable, and always willing to try new and different things. They possess a natural intuition but may also be easily led by others and should avoid overindulging in alcohol, drugs, and sex. In addition, those born on the 14th day of the month are self-determined, practical, reliable, and disciplined.

15: Those born on the 15th day of the month receive a mixed outcome of energies from the numbers 1, 5, and 6, with 1 being dominant while 5's energy depletes. They tend to be loyal and creative, with a special inclination towards music. Individuals born on this day have an instinctive ability to sense when someone needs emotional support and are usually the first to offer help. They are dynamic, adaptable, freedom-loving, and versatile in their approach towards life.

16: Individuals born on the 16th day of the month receive a mixed outcome of energies from the numbers 1, 6, and 7, with 1 being dominant while 6's energy depletes. They may find it difficult to express their thoughts and feelings and may prefer to retreat into themselves rather than confront potentially challenging situations. Those born on this day tend to be intellectual, spiritual, introspective, and analytical in their approach towards life.

17: Those born on the 17th day of the month receive a mixed outcome of energies from the numbers 1, 7, and 8, with 1 being dominant while 7's energy depletes. Individuals born on this day tend to be good with money and finances, working steadily towards their goals with great determination. They are ambitious, self-motivated, powerful, and determined in their pursuits, striving for success in all areas of life.

18: Individuals born on the 18th day of the month receive a mixed outcome of energies from the numbers 1, 8, and 9, with 1 being dominant while 8's energy depletes. They tend to be good administrators and natural humanitarians, with a talent for combining these qualities and making a career in philanthropic fields. Those born on this day are often characterised by their humanitarianism, responsibility, compassion, and selflessness in their interactions with others.

19: Individuals born on the 19th day of the month receive a mixed outcome of energies from the numbers 1, 9, and 1, with 1 being dominant while 9's energy depletes.

They are versatile individuals who prefer to work with as little interference from others as possible, but their emotions can sometimes let them down as they tend to be driven more by emotions than logic. Those born on this day are characterised by their leadership qualities, assertiveness, confidence, and independence in their pursuits.

20: Individuals born on the 20th day of the month are Cooperation, sensitivity, diplomacy, intuition, but because of the O's presence the 2's good quality depletes

21: Individuals born on the 21st day of the month receive a mixed outcome of energies from the numbers 2, 1, and 3, with 2 being dominant while 1's energy depletes. They are creative and expressive individuals who possess an optimistic outlook on life. They tend to be sociable and enjoy interacting with others. These individuals have a natural ability to see both sides of an argument and can often come up with creative solutions to problems.

22: Individuals born on the 22nd day of the month receive a mixed outcome of energies from the numbers 2 and 4, repeated 2 amplified Moon's moodiness . They are hardworking and practical, with excellent organisational skills. However, they may struggle with expressing their emotions and can sometimes be seen as reserved or detached.

23: Individuals born on the 23rd day of the month receive a mixed outcome of energies from the numbers 2, 3 and 5, with 2 being dominant while 3's energy depletes. They are naturally curious and adventurous, with a love for exploring new things and experiences. They are also adaptable and versatile, able to adjust to different situations and environments with ease.

24: People born on the 24th of the month are nurturing, responsible, and compassionate. They receive a mixed outcome of energies from the numbers 2, 4, and 6, with 2 being dominant while 4's energy depletes. They are often motivated and enthusiastic in their approach to achieving their goals, and place a strong emphasis on family and caring for others.

25: Individuals born on the 25th of any month are believed to inherit a combination of energies from the numbers 2, 5, and 7. While the energy of 2 is dominant, the influence of 5 is believed to wane. People born on this day are thought to possess traits such as intuition, gentleness, and a need for solitude. However, they may also be sensitive and may withdraw when hurt.

Additionally, they may exhibit analytical, intellectual, introspective, and spiritual tendencies.

26: Those born on the 26th are said to receive a blend of energies from the numbers 2, 6, and 8, with the energy of 2 being the most prominent. Traits such as intuition, gentleness, and a need for alone time are commonly associated with individuals born on this day, as well as sensitivity and a tendency to withdraw when feeling hurt. Furthermore, they may display analytical, intellectual, introspective, and spiritual tendencies. Additionally, ambition, authority, power, and determination are also traits that may be associated with those born on this day.

27: Individuals born on the 27th of any month are believed to receive a mixture of energies from the numbers 2, 7, and 9, with the energy of 2 being the strongest influence. People born on these days are often drawn to change and variety and enjoy taking on responsibility and serving others. They may also exhibit traits such as humanitarianism, compassion, idealism, and selflessness.

28: People born on the 28th of any month are believed to receive a blend of energies from the numbers 2, 8, and 1, with the energy of 2 being the most dominant. Traits such as resourcefulness, independence, determination, and confidence are commonly associated with individuals born on this day. They tend to prefer being in control and may not like being told what to do, often thriving when they are their own boss.

29: Those born on the 29th day of any month are believed to experience a combination of energies from the numbers 2 and 9, as well as the heightened potential of the number 11 (as 2+9=11). Individuals born on this day may possess traits such as intuition, sensitivity, vision, and spirituality.

30: Individuals born on the 30th day of any month are often characterised as intelligent, creative, and loving. However, the presence of the number 0 in their birthdate can mitigate some of the negative aspects of the number 3, which is a prominent influence on this day. People born on this day may also exhibit traits such as adaptability, sociability, expression, and versatility.

31: Those born on the 31st day of any month are thought to inherit a mixture of energies from the numbers 3, 1, and 4. Individuals born on this day may start from humble beginnings but have the potential to rise steadily through the ranks. Traits such as transformative abilities, regeneration, change, and upheaval may be associated with them.

Chapter 8

Zodiac signs, & Planets

This chapter goes into the relationship between the 12 zodiac signs and the numerology numbers that belong to them. Every zodiac sign has unique characteristics and qualities that are enhanced by their numerology number. Understanding the relationship between zodiac signs and numerology allows us to get a deeper understanding of ourselves and people around us. As we assigned each planet a number, we set up a relationship between zodiac sign as-well. The astrological world begins with a zodiac sign.

PLANET	SIGN NAME	SYMBOL
SUN	LEO	♌
MOON	CANCER	♋
JUPITER	SAGITTARIUS	♐
	PISCES	♓
MERCURY	GEMINI	♊
	VIRGO	♍
VENUS	TAURUS	♉
	LIBRA	♎
SATURN	CAPRICORN	♑
	AQUARIUS	♒
MARS	ARIES	♈
	SCORPIO	♏

Number 1 the Sun is associated with vitality, power, and creativity. It is our true selves and our life's purpose.

Leo (July 23-August 22) - number 1

Leo has a relationship with the practice of numerology number 1, new beginnings, leadership, and self-confidence. Those born under this sign are confident, charismatic individuals who value self-expression and creativity. Their passion and love of drama characterise them. 1 a pioneering and independent number. The number 1 in their numerology chart to be natural leaders who value independence and self-confidence.

Number 2 linked the Moon as emotions, intuition, and nurturing. It is our inner selves and our emotional needs.

Cancer (June 22-July 22) - number 2

Cancer is associated with the numerology number 2, which is balance, harmony, and partnership. Those born under this sign are reliable, practical individuals who value stability and security. Their patience and their love of comfort characterise them. Consider the number 2 a peaceful number. Those with the number 2 in their numerology chart remain as a peacemaker who value relationships and harmony.

Number 3, Jupiter is associated with growth, expansion, and luck. It is our opportunities for growth and abundance.

Sagittarius (November 22-December 21) - number 3

Sagittarius is a fire sign associated with the numerology number 3. People born under this sign are adventurous, optimistic, and humorous. Their love of travel, philosophical insights, and ability to see the bigger picture characterised them. 3 resonates with the energy of Sagittarius, as it is creativity and self-expression.

Pisces (February 19-March 20) - number 3

Pisces is a water sign associated with the numerology number 3. People born under this sign are empathetic, intuitive, and compassionate. Creativity characteristics, artistic talents, and their ability to connect with others on an emotional level shows their quality. The number 3 resonates with the energy of Pisces, as it is creativity, self-expression, and communication.

Number 5 Mercury is associated with conversation, intelligence, and versatility. It is our skill to communicate and make connections.

Gemini (May 21-June 21) - number 5

Gemini is an air sign linked to the numerology number 5. Their intellectual curiosity, versatility, and sociable nature characterise those born under this sign. They are often excellent communicators and skilled at adapting to different conditions. The number 5 resonates with the energy of Gemini, as it represents change and freedom, essential for their personal growth.

Virgo (August 23-September 22) - number 5

Virgo is an earth sign associated with the numerology number 5. Their analytical mind, attention to detail, and practical approach to life characterise those born under this sign. They are often hardworking and strive for perfection in everything they do. The number 5 resonates with the energy of Virgo, as it represents change and adaptability, important for achieving their goals.

Number 6 Venus is associated with love, good looks, and pleasure. It represents our ability to attract and enjoy the good things in life.

Taurus (April 20-May 20) - number 6

Taurus is an earth sign associated with the numerology number 6. Practicality, stability, and love of comfort characterise people born under this sign. They are often dependable, grounded, and they value security through stability in life. The number 6 resonates with the energy of Taurus, as it represents nurturing and compassion, essential for their emotional well-being.

Libra (September 23-October 23) - number 6

Libra is an air sign associated with the numerology number 6. People born under this sign are characterised by their diplomatic nature, charm, desire for balance and harmony in all aspects of life. They are often excellent mediators who strive to create a peaceful and harmonious environment. The number 6 resonates with the energy of Libra, as it is balance and harmony, which are essential for their inner harmony.

Number 8 Saturn is the sixth celestial body from the sun and is known as the "Ringed Planet" because of its distinctive ring system. In astrology, Saturn is connected with discipline, responsibility, and restriction. It symbolises our commitment and the obstacles we must confront to progress and become better people.

Capricorn (December 22 - January 19) - number 8

Capricorn is an earth sign associated with Saturn. Their ambition, practicality, and strong work ethic characterise people born under this sign. We often see them as dependable, responsible, as they have a natural ability to lead and organise. Saturn's influence on Capricorn manifest as a strong sense of duty and responsibility and a want for achievement and success.

Aquarius (January 20 - February 18) - number 8

Aquarius is an air sign associated with Saturn. Their independent nature, humanitarianism, and innovative thinking characterises people born under this sign. We often see them as intellectual, unconventional, as they have a strong want to create positive change in the world.

Saturn's influence on Aquarius manifest as a wish for stability through personal freedom and autonomy.

Number 9 Mars often refer to as the "Red Planet" because of its reddish character. In astrology, Mars is associated with energy, passion, and action.

Aries (March 21 - April 19) - number 9

Aries is a fire sign associated with Mars. Their courage, energy, and competitiveness characterise people born under this sign. They are often seen as natural leaders because of their desire to take action. The impact of Mars on Aries manifests an impetuous character, a longing for independence and freedom, and a drive for excitement and adventure.

Scorpio (October 24 - November 21) - number 9

Scorpio is a water sign associated with Mars. Their intensity, passion, and emotional depth characterises people born under this sign. We often see them as mysterious and powerful, and they have a strong want to uncover the truth and expose hidden realities. Scorpio's Mars influence emerge as a drive for control and power, a yearning for transformation and rebirth, and a willingness to take risks in order to attain their goals.

Chapter 9

Personality Number

Adding and reducing the day of birth calculates a person's personality number. In some books, or resources, an online search engine may refer to Personality, Psychic, Birthday, Driver, Mul-ank, or Primary number.

Birthday number governs an individual's personality, and for easier understanding, we call it a personality number in this book.

The personality number provides a glimpse into an individual's inner self, who they are, what they desire, and how they relate to the outside world.

NOTE: The numbers linked to your date of birth, day, month, and year are not changeable, as we do with name.

The date, time, and location of our birth influences our mental constitution, shaping our perception of ourselves from the very first breath. Our birth determines this unique composition, which in turn reflects in our personality number, governing our food preferences, approach to romantic relationships, friendships, and even marriage, as well as our aspirations, desires, and needs.

The sum of the digits that make up the day of your birth is used to calculate birthday number. But, when your two digits number becomes either 11 OR 22, please write as 11/2, and 22/4.

Refer the Numbers chapter to memorise the masters number, and the what they signify.

The formula for numerology number calculation is referred as Reducing Number.

19 is 1 (1 + 9 = 10; 1 + 0 = 1)

28 is 1 (2 + 8 = 10; 1 + 0 = 1)

29 is 2 (2 + 9 = 11; 1 + 1 = 2)

Calculating Personality Number		
Birthday	Formula	Single Digit
10 JUL	1 + 0	1
16 JAN	1 + 6	7
29 JUN	2 + 9 = 11 = 11	11/2

P1 (1st, 10th, 19th, or 28th)

The planet SUN controls the personality number ONE (1), and the person with personality number (1) desires to become a superior leader, manager who is self-ruling, ambitious, and creative and not scared to take risks remarkable in the throng. Sun-ruled personalities always fixate on their goals and ideas, appearing kind, royal, disciplined, authoritative, strong, original, and kinglike.

They are confident and dislike interfering with their commute to work. They take pleasure in taking control and leading others, and they are most joyful when they are in control or have the freedom to put into practice their own thoughts. They may also relish observing others.

They want to be on top to start a different activity or task. These people are best suited for politics and higher-level organisational positions since they are skilled at making friends and socialising.

POSITIVE

Independent, Creative, Leaders, Creators

NEGATIVE

Egoistic, Arrogant, Domineering, Anger

P2 (2nd, 11th, 20th, or 29th)

A personality number TWO (2), led by the MOON, controls the mind. A personality number (2) reflects someone who excels in a team-oriented setting and enjoys working in the background. Sensitivity, thoughtfulness, and a communal attitude are all normal characteristics. Moon-ruled people are queenlike, royal, attractive, ever-changing, and delicate, giving them tenderness, artistic inclinations, and a romantic character.

There is a sense of peace and gentleness about them.It is their imaginative nature that makes them inventive, but it lacks determination and they not execute their ideas forcefully. They are are often thought to have a deep emotional nature, be compassionate and nurturing towards others, possess an intuitive ability to perceive the feelings of those around them, and have a strong attachment to their family and home.

POSITIVE

Duality, Peaceful, Co-operative, Builder

NEGATIVE

Nagging, Fault-finding, Worried, Susceptible

P3 (3rd, 12th, 21st or 30th)

The planet JUPITER represents the personality number of THREE (3). A 3rd birthday person is known for their originality, energy friendliness and a comical side. As a result of Jupiter ruling, people are spiritual, counselling, friendly, self-centered, disciplined, and independent. They are also bold, active, dependable and hard-working. There is a great deal of ambition in personal number 3 people.

Their goal is to get ahead in their field. As far as their lives go, they want to make a lasting impression so that they will be remembered by future generations. Their future-oriented nature makes them very forward-looking. Their second virtue is their attractiveness. They talk your way to the top since they have remarkable conversational skills.They are appreciated for their cheerfulness, outgoingness, animation, expressiveness, imagination, and creativity in their interactions.

POSITIVE

Joyous, Cheerful, Expressional, Comport

NEGATIVE

Sensual, Selfish, Scattering, Impatient

P4 (4th, 13th, 22nd or 31st)

The planet RAHU/URANUS stands for the character number FOUR (4). An individual with the birthday figure 4 is usually sensible, reliable, industrious, honest, equitable, and self-controlled. Personality 4 persons are rebellious, impulsive, irritable, and secretive. Rahu and Ketu, the Moon's two nodes, reflect man's underlying bipolar character. They do not exist as physical entities in the same way that the other seven planets do. They each indicate a point where the Moon's orbit around our planet crosses with the ecliptic of the zodiac constellation.

They view everything from a totally unique angle, who view everything from the same angle. In every disagreement, they argue from the opposing side, and as a result, they amass many secret opponents. They despise laws, legal frameworks and seek to destroy. They always oppose the king and build their own kingdoms.

POSITIVE

Builders, Materialistic, Intellectual, Analytical

NEGATIVE

Critical, Self-limited, Economical, Low-spirited

P5 (5th, 14th, or 23rd)

The planet MERCURY stands for the identity number FIVE (5). The number 5 described as adventurous and flourish in changing places. A person having a 5th birthday is considered as magnetic and attracted to the opposite sex.

Those born under the sign of Mercury are royal, entertaining, cunning, astute, and sensitive. Mercury, the smallest planet in our solar system, is known for its quick response, changeable personality, ready wit, and restlessness. It is known as an evergreen planet, or a world that is young. Despite their inconsistency, they are savvy and sharp, and they gravitate towards fields where they may make quick money, avoiding the risky and arduous paths. They take quick decisions.

POSITIVE

Smart, Adaptable, Learned, Resilient, Analytical, Attractive to opposite sex

NEGATIVE

Greediness, Money-minded, Calculative, Careless, Restless, Impulsive

P6 (6th, 15th, or 24th)

The planet VENUS is the personality number SIX (6). A person with a birthday number of 6 is artistic and idealistic, and they enjoy comforting and nurturing people. Other characteristics include strong familial ties, a responsible temperament, and a profound affection for children and animals. Those born under the sign of Venus are amorous, slow, sensual, sweet-talkative, diplomatic, manipulative, active, artistic, sensual, and passionate.

They are always looking for harmony and love in their relationships with others, offering understanding, stability, trust, loyalty, and a readiness to take on responsibilities. These people are youthful, kind, eloquent, luxurious, creative, and have sophisticated taste. They are easily attracted to individuals of the opposite sex and are usually appreciated and respected by them.

POSITIVE

Guardians, Homely, Luxury, Friendly, Musical

NEGATIVE

Anxious, Self-esteem, Care Seeker, Involvement in the affairs of others, Argues, Domestic or sexual exploitation

P7 (7th, 16th or 25th)

The planet KETU/NEPTUNE is the personality number SEVEN (7). A person with the birthday number 7 is analytical in their decision making, as well as private and caring. Ketu controls those who are mystical, dreamy, intuitive, innovative, and thirsty for true knowledge.

It gives intellect, discriminating power, and psychic powers to its inhabitants. Ketu natives are vocal; they enjoy conversations avoid disputes. They live in their fantasies, are intuitive and inventive, and enjoy exaggerating. In their interactions with others, they are quiet and secretive. Individuals ruled by numerology number 7 are often associated with being introspective, analytical, spiritual, and possessing a deep desire for knowledge and understanding of the world around them.

POSITIVE

Wisdom, Research, Knowledge, Spiritual, Dignified, Educator, Intuitive, Nature lover

NEGATIVE

Distant, Restless, Stubborn, Opinionated, Unpredictable, Skeptical, Unapproachable

P8 (8th, 17th or 26th)

The planet SATURN is the personality number EIGHT (8). A person with the birthday number 8 is wise for money, judgement, and huge initiatives. They support their ambition, confidence, and authority. People born under the sign of Saturn are wise, malevolent, servant, laborious, struggling, suffering, wrong, sincerity, honesty, love of justice, non-attachment, long-life, fame, authority, leadership, and organisational ability.

Misunderstanding brings them mental suffering and becomes isolated, but they embrace spirituality. It applies to both the material and spiritual sides of life. This number is revolutions, anarchy, earthquakes, and many wicked and unusual happenings. This number influences philosophy, religion, and determination. They believe they are distinct from the rest and so unique.

POSITIVE

Spiritual, Material things, Large executive, Diplomat

NEGATIVE

Power demonstration, Unappreciative, Merciless driver

P9 (9th, 18th or 27th)

The planet MARS is the personality number of NINE (9). A person with the birthday number 9 usually exhibits generosity, open-mindedness, sensitivity, creativity, and provide original solutions to issues. This birthday number is frequently associated with humanitarianism.

Mars-ruled people are warlike, strong, gruff, rustic, perfectionist, doubting, fighting, alienating, discriminating, and always busy. They are ambitious and make rapid progress on their chosen route because of their strong will and determination. They react to events and become attentive at the first sign of trouble. They are arbitrators and will never become slaves to anyone. They may sustain financial or combat wounds. They are brave and make excellent soldiers. Their self-love is the primary source of their adversity. They dislike receiving counsel. They enjoy being powerful in their personal lives.

POSITIVE

Humanitarian, Action driven, Artistic, Sympathy

NEGATIVE

Selfish, Miserly, Destructive, Anger

MASTER NUMBERS

A master number is a two-digit number that repeats itself. Those with a master number (11th or 22nd) in their chart born with additional spiritual essence.

Reduce the number 11 to a master number, and the reduced number is 2 (1 + 1 = 2), which is a root number.

P11 (11th, 29th)

People refer to the 11/2 as the spiritual messenger. An 11/2 is perceived as intuitive, sympathetic, and too exuberant, as well as inspiring. Other characteristics include a wish to lead and the ability to bring peace and harmony to a tense situation. All of these properties are said to be among the highest vibrations of the 11/2. The 11/2 might be overwhelmed by dread or they might challenge themselves to achieve great things. As a result, the 11/2 is shown wrestling between self-destruction and greatness.

POSITIVE

Inspirational, Enthusiastic, Dynamic, Divinity

NEGATIVE

Miserly, Lacking self-esteem

P22 (22nd)

TWENTY-TWO: The 22/4 master builder is often a planner, builder, and outstanding visionary with the capacity to perceive the "big picture" without losing sight of all the vital tiny aspects. A 22/4 be the driving force behind big projects since they are good organisers and hard workers. The 22/4 is also connected with idealism, intuition, confidence, and knowledge.

Because of the lesser vibration of this number, the 22/4 become overwhelmed and overworked, especially if they are in the midst of a number of big endeavours. As a result, a 22/4 must pay particular attention to achieving a healthy work-life balance.

POSITIVE

Practical, Inspirational, Corporation heads

NEGATIVE

Big talkers, Proud, Egotism

Chapter 10

Life Path Number

Life path number derived through adding the digits of the birth date, month, and year until we obtain a single digit number. If the total comes to 11 or 22, we stop further reducing and write as 11/2, 22/4.

The life path number known as Destiny, Conductor, and Bhagya Ank number.

The life path number is one of the most important numerological calculations, as it provides a blueprint for a person's journey through life. This number is often seen as a guide or a map that helps individuals navigate the ups and downs of life, make better choices, and discover their true potential. It is also believed that each life path number has its own unique set of challenges and opportunities, and understanding these help people make the most of their lives.

As the name suggests, the destiny number is paramount in the numerology world, as because it shows our life's purpose. It shows us the right route throughout our life. Using the Life Path Number with the other numbers in your numerology assists us in navigating the twists and turns yet to appear life's route.

We have little idea as what we should do with our lives, thus examining the Life Path number guides us in the relevant income source, connection, and wealth bringing.

The Life Path number offers information on one's natural talents and aptitudes, which be useful when deciding on a life path. As a result, in circles, we regard the Life Path number as the most essential of the numbers in one's numerology profile.

The life path number is a crucial factor in numerology that tells a person's core personality traits, strengths, weaknesses, and life purpose. We calculate it by adding the digits in a person's birth date and reducing them to a single digit. We believe this number to offer insight into a person's life journey and the lessons they need to learn.

The life number becomes active between the ages of 27 and 30 and it shows the purpose of an individual's life. The number shows that one has to work for the level of self- development.

Consider the Life Path number as a navigation map leading you through the journey of life, guiding you through your life's goal.

Understanding your life path number help you make better decisions regarding your career, relationships, and personal growth. It   guide you in finding your true purpose in life and fulfilling your potential. In numerology, we consider the life path number a valuable tool for self-discovery and personal development.

We consider eleven life path numbers: 1, 2, 3, 4, 5, 6, 7, 8, 9, 11, and 22, Eleven and Twenty-two known as master number and bring in added energy and spiritual awareness.

Analysing a man born on Oct 21, 1981.

Life Path Calculation

STEP1		
DD	MM	YYYY
21	10	1981

STEP2 (Addition)
2+1+1+1+9+8+1 = 23

STEP3 (Reduce)
2+3 = 5

The Life-path number is FIVE (5) for Oct 21, 1981

Special Note: If you arrive to either 11 or 22 at the step2, please confirm if it's a master number as below:

- *Identify the number for the month of birth. January =1, February = 2, March = 3, April = 4, May = 5, June = 6, July = 7, August = 08, September = 09, October = 10, November = 11, and December = 12*

STEP2 (Add Digits)	
MONTH	10
DAY	21
YEAR	1981
TOTAL	2012

STEP3 (Reduce)
2+1+2 = 5

- *Add all the digits together and finally reduce to a single digit*

- *If the calculated number become either 11 or 22, please refer the special note.*

Life Path awakens the individual's specific interests, unique abilities, attitudes, talents, and guides him to the purpose of one's being on Earth.

1 Life Path

Independence is the perfect word to describe the 1 life path number.

People with the life path number 1 must learn to stand independent and meet their goals. They may appear dependent until the age of 27-30, but they become independent and remain pioneers in the latter half of their lives. As they grow, they become trend-makers, originators, and influencers in the end.

As individual moves forward, they gain higher levels, superior positions, and improved life steadiness. The Sun is the originator planet, and its vigour levels the Aura, thus the number One (1) carries on to bolster the planet's power and so they thrive despite obstacles.

Their inquisitive minds, in addition to administrative qualities and executive capabilities, propel them to a higher position with authority in their sector. They need to attend to their crucial personal needs.

They prepare for any outward activities with a brilliant head, and they appreciate a bigger, lighter, and more joyful life. They are bold pioneers and respect individuality.

Their arrogance, grandiosity, and domineering egotism become a challenge over time, since others perceive them as domineering. Because 1's often become bored by routine, they may act too soon to avoid falling. Many struggle to gain independence and appear reliant. They might strive to build themselves up by tearing others.

CAREER AND BUSINESS

They appreciate activities and organisations that distinguish them. Here are some of the top job and business opportunities for people with Life Path 1:

Entrepreneurship: Because of their inherent leadership abilities and entrepreneurial zeal, 1 people frequently thrive at founding and running their own businesses. They see and are determined to see it through, and will take calculated risks to achieve their objectives.

Leadership Positions: Leadership positions are great for Life Path 1 persons who enjoy being in charge and making decisions that affect the organisation. They have a natural ability to inspire and motivate others, as well as set goals and methods for success.

Politics or Public Service: Wanting to have an impact on the world, jobs in politics or public service may be a good fit for 1 person.

Law or Legal Representation: Many have a natural talent for legal representation and work in law or other similar disciplines. They have a strong sense of what is right and wrong and utilise their leadership skills to fight for fairness and protect everyone's rights.

Business or Financial Analysis Jobs: Jobs in business or financial analysis be perfect for them as they possess a natural knack for strategic planning and problem-solving. They analyse data, identify opportunities for growth, improvement, and make smart decisions based on their findings.

Engineering and Technology: With their natural talent for invention, resolving issues, jobs in engineering, technology be an ideal match for 1 individuals. They relish designing, building new products, systems, apply leadership abilities to control and inspire teams of engineers and designers.

Exercise or Fitness: Life Path 1 individuals delight in challenging themselves as they have a natural athleticism and enjoy competing at the highest levels.

2 Life Path

Collaboration, harmony, and serenity depict the number Two (2).

Those born along the journey of life (2) are cooperative, helpful, modest, neat, tactful, and diplomatic.

People with a two destiny number puts others at ease. They appear cordial and charming, and they make excellent hosts and hostesses. They are sensitive and make new friends. They would rather be in a long-term relationship than be alone. By nature, they are gentle, peaceful, and perceptive. They set up good friends and communicate. They are unconcerned their social standing or material demands.

As a result, they usually find themselves as the secondary leader builder rather than the leader.

The drive to comprehend people and have a spiritual understanding of the universe is consistent with 2. Generally, people look upon those with this fortune number than peacemakers and intercessors, which is why they usually regard them as adept at facing tricky predicaments.

Those with a life path of 2 are also said to be inspirational and capable of leading by example. Individuals with this number are well suited for occupations as teachers, social workers, philosophers, and advisors due to these qualities. This number also has a strong spiritual component, making its owners more likely to operate with ideal notions than those that manufacture material prosperity.

Moon is regarded as the planet of the mind, and life path 2 represents the celestial body, and these people strive to balance their minds for a serene existence. They have a decent financial situation, but they tend to jump from one job to the next, causing delays in completion.

CAREER AND BUSINESS

They draw on jobs and enterprises that include people to meet common objectives.

Advice or Therapy: Because of their inherent empathy and ability to connect with others, occupations in advising or therapy may be a good fit for Life Path 2 people. They have a gift for hearing, offering help, help people discuss their problems and find answers.

Teaching or tutoring: Jobs in teaching or tutoring are excellent choices for your Life Path. 2. Working in a group helps kids learn and grow. They show a talent for communication, offer a supportive and encouraging learning environment.

Social Work or Community Outreach: Careers in social work or community outreach fit their desire to assist others.

Diplomacy or Mediation: With their ability to collaborate, find common ground, careers in diplomacy or mediation be a great fit. They navigate complex relationships and negotiate solutions that benefit all parties.

Creative Arts: Careers in the creative arts, such as writing, music, or visual arts be a great success for 2 individuals who have a natural talent for creativity and expression.

Human Resources or Management: Careers in human resources or management be a great fit for life path 2 individuals who enjoy working with others creating a positive and supportive work environment. They have a natural talent for communication and creates a culture of collaboration through teamwork.

Nonprofit or Charity Work: Career in nonprofit or charity work be a great fit as-well.

3 Life Path

The word self-expression best describes 3 life path number.

Creativity, optimism, inspiration, and a want to live to the fullest depict a Life Path 3 person. As a result, they drew to occupations in writing, speaking, singing, acting, or teaching.

Those with the number 3 must express themselves. Because this manifestation involves verbal abilities, it might encompass singing, talking, or writing. Threes are superb conversationalists, and their strength is communication. They have lively, imaginative brains that are buzzing with ideas. But, they lack the motivation to put them to use.

They place a high emphasis on friendships; as a result, they stay loyal to friends. Because of the social spirit of 3, Jupiter is the governing planet. These individuals are cheerful, humorous the entertainer, enthusiastic, skilled at writing, speaking, and singing, prefer to be happier, enjoy children, and are self-expressive.

These individuals are often drawn to spiritual or philosophical pursuits and have a deep desire to understand the mysteries of life. Overall, the combination of the life path number 3 and the planet Jupiter represents a powerful force for personal growth, creativity, and expansion.

CAREER AND BUSINESS

They often pursue occupations and firms that permit them to employ their abilities to motivate and amuse others.

Bringing out their charisma and enjoying self-expression: Acting or performing may be an ideal occupation for people who have a life path 3, as they are charismatic and enjoy expressing themselves. They enjoy being in the spotlight and bring their unique talents and perspectives to the stage or screen.

Using their inherent creativity and enjoyment of self-expression, careers in writing or journalism be a great fit for 3 individuals. They communicate their ideas, perspectives in a compelling and engaging manner.

Occupations in art or design: Occupations in art or design be a great match for them who have a natural aptitude for inventiveness and beauty. They enjoy using their artistic skills to create and inspiring works of art, and bring their unique vision to life.

Communications or Advertising: With their natural charisma and ability to communicate, careers in communications or advertising be a great fit for 3 individuals. They have a talent for creating compelling messages and promote products and services in a way that inspires and engages others.

Selling or Business Expansion: With their innate charisma and magnetism, professions in selling or business expansion be an ideal match for life path 3 people. They enjoy building relationships with others and use their persuasive skills to close deals and achieve business objectives.

Tutoring or Instruction: Careers in tutoring or instruction be a great fit for 3 individuals who take pleasure in passing on their knowledge and stimulating others to learn and develop. They have a natural talent for communication and create engaging and interactive learning experiences.

Entrepreneurship: Employing their innate creativity and love of self-expression, entrepreneurship be a great fit for life path 3 individuals. They enjoy using their talents to create innovative products and services, and inspire and motivate others to join them in pursuit of their vision.

4 Life Path

The word practice, order, and routine best describes 4 life path number.

People with a life path number of 4 must work hard. They are realistic, dependable, attentive, and well-organised individuals who appreciate following routines. They bring order out of chaos. The workers take pleasure in seeing the fruits of their labor. Fours will trudge along for years if they   see that the work is worthwhile. They are detail-oriented and like fine, complex work. They are stiff and stubborn people who find it difficult to change their ideas after they have made up their minds.

These individuals display discipline, family orientation, hard work, honesty, organisation, patience, patriotism, practicality, and dependability.

4 corresponds to the demand for order, service, and management. This, along with a good dose of patience and thoroughness, makes them ideal for a job in construction, engineering, and handicraft, as well as any industry that values planning, organising, regulating, and following a routing.

The planet Rahu / Uranus rules the number 4, and 4s have such high expectations, those who not meet these expectations disappoint or disillusion them. They get along best with those who are realistic, decent, and fulfilled by doing good for others.

CAREER AND BUSINESS

They often drawn to professions and ventures that require organisation, and a strong work ethic. Here are a few career and business options for Life path 4 individuals:

Accounting or Finance: because of their meticulousness and affinity for organisation, careers in accounting or finance be a great fit for life path 4 individuals. They have a talent for numbers and are able to create efficient and effective financial systems.

Jobs in engineering or architecture: Jobs in engineering or architecture be a great fit for 4 individuals, who have a natural talent for constructing practical and designs. They enjoy problem-solving and create solutions that are both efficient and pleasing.

Occupations in Project Management: With their innate capacity to arrange and organise, occupations in project management be an ideal match for them. They enjoy taking a structured approach to achieving goals and lead teams to success.

Employment in Administration or Operations: Employment in administration or operations be a great fit for 4 individuals, who have a knack for constructing systems and processes that are efficient and successful. They enjoy ensuring that everything runs and find and discuss inefficiencies.

Law or Government: With their natural respect for rules and regulations, careers in law or government be a great fit for life path 4 individuals. They enjoy working within a structured environment and navigate complex legal or regulatory environments.

Manufacturing or Construction: Careers in manufacturing or construction be a great fit for 4 individuals who have a gift for crafting practical items or structures. They enjoy working with their hands and bring their designs to life.

Health and Safety: With their natural respect for rules and regulations, careers in health and safety be a great fit for them. They enjoy ensuring that systems are safe and effective and find and discuss potential risks.

5 Life Path

The words liberty, experience, and movement best describe 5 life path number.

They are Versatile, Bold, Engaging, Intelligent, Independent, Sociable, Great marketers, Wry, Globetrotters, drawn to physical attraction, liberty, seeks progress, and leads an equilibrium lifestyle are qualities of individuals born under the sign of Five (5). We consider the 5 a harmonious, magical number;

They are likely to explore early in life, but once they discover their actual course, they accomplish a great deal. These people are always inquisitive, enthusiastic, and young at heart.

Multi-talented and adaptive nature comes with the life figure 5, as the ruling planet Mercury shows vitality on those people. As a result, they posses ability to perform multiple things at the same time.

Overindulgence is a bad for them. These people change their minds and find it difficult to commit to anything for an extended period. Many people experiment with and abuse alcohol, drugs, and sex.

This person must be proficient at communicating ideas and comprehend how to interact with others. When these skills are combined with the attributes of a number 5, this individual is well-suited for a job in advertising, sales, or entertainment. Restlessness is usual in people with this predestined number, and it prevent them from remaining with any undertaking or pursuit for long periods of time.

CAREER AND BUSINESS

They often draw on careers and businesses that involve travel, excitement, and change. Here are some of the best career and business options for Life path 5 individuals:

Entrepreneurship: With their love of freedom and willingness to take risks, 5 individuals often thrive in entrepreneurial ventures. They enjoy being their own boss and pursuing their own creative ideas.

Sales or Marketing: Many have a natural talent for persuasion and enjoy careers in sales or marketing. They connect with others and sell products or services in a way that feels authentic and compelling.

Travel or Hospitality: Careers in travel or hospitality be a great as they enjoy exploring new places and meeting new people. They excel at creating welcoming and engaging environments that make others feel at home.

Photography or Videography: With their love of visual stimulation and creative expression, careers in photography or videography be a great fit for life path 5 individuals. They have a talent for capturing the essence of a moment and telling stories through images.

Journalism or Broadcasting: Many Life path 5 individuals enjoy careers in journalism or broadcasting, where they   use their natural curiosity and communication skills to inform and entertain others. They have a gift for storytelling and connect with audiences meaningfully.

Fitness or Sports: Careers in fitness or sports be a great fit as they enjoy staying active and pushing themselves to their limits. They have a natural athleticism and enjoy challenging themselves.

Real Estate or Property Management: With their love of change and variety, careers in real estate or property management be a great fit for life path 5 individuals. They enjoy helping others find new homes or spaces to explore and navigate the complexities of the real estate market with ease.

6 Life Path

The words luxury, home, and family best describe 6 life path number.

Individuals with the life path number 6 are nurturing, kind, and responsible. They appreciate bearing other people's troubles and lending a shoulder to others. They take great pleasure in assisting those they care.

When things are not going well, they become family members. Sixes make sure that everyone is satisfied with the outcome of interpersonal conflicts. Their friends and loved ones surround them and make them happier. They are sympathetic and kind. Sixes are inventive, especially in the arts. People with this number are more likely to be artistic, domestic, humanitarian, musical, nurturing, responsible, serving, and teachers.

This life path strives for responsibility, love, balance, helpful, conscientious, and capable of resolving a controversial issue. These qualities make the the life path number 6 ideal for occupations working with the elderly, young, sick, and poor.

Close family bonds and a comfortable home life are important to those with number 6. They are excellent parents who are interested in household activities. Medicine, social work, teaching, religious life, and home construction are all popular careers outside the home.

The planet Venus is the governing planet of the number 6, yet it is uncommon for someone to use their 6 life path. Everyone else's difficulties frequently overwhelmed sixes who assume everyone's obligations.

CAREER AND BUSINESS

They are regularly attracted to occupations and businesses that involve assisting people, encouraging harmony, and producing beauty in the world. Here are some of the best career and business options for Life Path 6 individuals:

Counselling or Therapy: With their natural empathy and nurturing tendencies, 6 individuals are well-suited for careers in counselling or therapy. They understand others well and skilled at providing support and guidance.

Teaching or Education: Many Life Path 6 individuals find fulfilment in careers that involve teaching or educating. They have a passion for learning and enjoy sharing their knowledge. This could include careers in teaching, coaching, and mentoring.

Creative Arts: 6 individuals have a strong artistic streak and enjoy careers in the creative arts, writing, music, or visual arts. They have a natural eye for elegance and often drawn to careers to express creativity.

Hospitality and Event Planning: With their desire to create harmonious and welcoming environments, careers in hospitality or event planning be a great fit. They excel at creating a warm and inviting atmosphere and are skilled at anticipating the needs of others.

Social Work or Community Outreach: Life Path 6 individuals have a deep desire to serve others and promote social justice. Careers in social work or community outreach be a great fit for those with a Life Path 6, as they have a natural ability to connect with others and promote positive change.

Entrepreneurship: 6 individuals may find fulfilment in starting their own business, particularly if the business involves helping others or promoting wellness and harmony. This could include businesses in the areas of health and wellness, hospitality, or community outreach.

7 Life Path

Research, education, and analysis are the words describes the 7 life path number.

Individuals with a life path number of 7 require solitude to increase their understanding and skill. They take a distinct, one-of-a-kind approach to everything they carry out. This gives them originality, but it makes it difficult for them to evolve and adapt. It makes it hard for them to settle in a group setting.

Sevens prefer smaller circles of friends to giant circles of friends. They be challenging to comprehend at first because they secure themselves with defences, but they make wonderful friends once they trust the other person.

Life path number is associated with introspective, solitary, dignified, educator, intuitive, nature lover, silent, spiritual or scientific, and studious.

They are drawn to activities that require thought and study. They are deep thinkers, withdrawn, and aloof. They are also believed to be specialists in the field they specialise in.

Those with a 7 have a preference for working alone at their own pace, and they have difficulty expressing - or understanding their emotions. Perfectionists are sensible people who apply logic to everything they do.

People on the negative side of their 7 life path find it difficult connecting others so prefer to isolate themselves. They become more self-centred and introverted.

CAREER AND BUSINESS

They often draw on vacation, companies that involve research, analysis, and problem-solving.

Science or Research: With their analytical, and explorative mind, 7 individuals are well-suited for careers in science or research. They enjoy delving into intricate problems, finding solutions through analysis and experimentation.

Computing: Careers in computing be a great fit for 7 individuals, who often have a natural aptitude for understanding and working with complex systems. They enjoy learning about new technologies using them to solve problems and improve efficiency.

Writing or Journalism: Many have a natural talent for writing and enjoy careers in writing or journalism. They have a gift for research and analysis, and communicate complex ideas in a clear and compelling way.

Psychology or Counselling: Careers in psychology or counselling be a great fit for those who have a deep interest in understanding the human psyche through self-awareness and personal growth.

Education or Training: With their love of learning, gathering knowledge, careers in education or training be a great fit for 7 individuals. They enjoy sharing their knowledge and helping others to develop their own intellectual abilities.

Finance or Accounting: Many of them enjoy careers in finance or accounting. They have a natural ability to analyse and interpret financial data.

Consulting or Analysis: Careers in consulting or analysis be a great fit life path 7 individuals who enjoy solving complex problems and providing strategic guidance to businesses or organisations. They see patterns, connections that others may miss, hence skilled at identifying opportunities for growth and improvement.

8 Life Path

8 life path number is best described by the terms materialism, judgement, and efficiency.

Individuals with the life path number 8 enjoy large-scale enterprises and seek to help from their success. They set high standards for themselves and strive hard to carry out them. They are determined and ambitious, and they always succeed. We ground eights in reality and do not have time to daydream.

8s are ambitious, athletic, and efficient, with executive skills, sound judgement, and stamina.

This life path is associated with material wealth and financial security, as well as great project planning, initiation, and completion talents. It is important not to misinterpret this determination as intransigence or avarice.

They are often natural leaders who are not afraid of taking risks or making difficult decisions. However, the influence of Saturn also make them cautious and pragmatic, which means they tend to approach their endeavours in a methodical and deliberate manner. If they navigate in undesirable activities, they may make wealth, but at the expense of their health, happiness, and relationships. They have the potential to become intolerant, spiteful, and power-hungry.

CAREER AND BUSINESS

They love jobs and businesses involving power, influence, and financial success.

Business Management: Because of their inherent leadership qualities and financial intelligence, 8 persons excel in business management occupations. They appreciate taking leadership and develop and implementing strategic plans that lead to financial success.

Entrepreneurship: With their inherent ambition and financial savvy, life path 8 persons excel at entrepreneurship. They appreciate taking risks and build profitable businesses with high financial returns.

Finance or investment banking careers be a good fit for 8 people who have a natural knack for financial analysis and strategic planning. They appreciate dealing with numbers, devise and carry out investment plans that result in financial success.

Real estate occupations be a good fit for them because of their inherent want and financial aptitude. They enjoy dealing with real estate, hence explore and execute profitable real estate transactions.

Law or Corporate Law: Because of their inherent ambition and leadership characteristics, as they may be well-suited to jobs in law or corporate law. They enjoy working in a structured environment.

Executive Management: Because of their inherent leadership qualities and financial acumen, 8 persons may be well-suited to professions in senior management. They appreciate working in a structured corporate setting developing, implementing a strategic initiatives that result in financial success.

Politics or government: Because of their inherent want and leadership qualities, they could excel in careers in politics or government. They thrive in a structured political policy and negotiate difficult political contexts.

Those with Life path 8 succeed in occupations, businesses that need power, influence, and financial success. They have a natural talent for leadership, financial analysis, strategic planning and well managing a project.

9 Life Path

Humanitarianism, selflessness, and understanding are the best words to describe the 9 life path number.

People with the life path number 9 prone to self-sacrifice. They are sensitive, loving individuals who have a strong desire to serve assisting others and give rather than receive. As a result, they are exploitable, devastated when their deep and sincere love was not returned.

People with the life path number nine (9) exhibit artistic abilities, brotherly love, compassion, drama, philanthropy, and selflessness. This number is associated with compassion, good deeds, and awareness of others' needs. As a result, someone with this number must be eager to work hard and to encourage others. People with this number are innovative, creative, artistic, and they love their friendships.

Those with Life Path number 9 must use extreme caution to avoid being selfish or self-entered, which might occur if their personal objectives take precedence over those of the greater good.

They have a strong sense of justice and a desire to make a positive impact on the world. The influence of

Mars makes them assertive and independent. However, they must stay careful and maintain their aggression.

CAREER AND BUSINESS

They are frequently drawn to occupations and businesses that allow them to help others, promote social justice, and exhibit their creativity. Here are some of the top job and business opportunities for those with Life path 9:

Non-Profit or Charitable Work: Because of their innate humanitarian character, 9 persons excel in non-profit or charity work. They enjoy assisting people and have the ability to effect positive change in the world.

Careers in social work or counselling be a good fit for them due to their innate emotional intelligence. They appreciate assisting others and have an emotional connection with others.

Art or Creative Work: Because of their inherent inventiveness, 9 persons may be well-suited to careers in art or creative work. They like to express themselves and produce works of art that inspire others.

Writing or Journalism: Because of their inherent creativity and humanitarian spirit, as they may excel in writing or journalism occupations. They enjoy telling stories and develop works that raise awareness of social justice concerns.

Education or Teaching: Because of their innate desire to serve others and promote good change, 9 persons may excel in education or teaching. They appreciate imparting their knowledge and connect with pupils on a personal level.

Healing or Alternative Medicine: Because of their innate desire to serve others and promote healing, life path 9 persons may excel in occupations in healing or alternative medicine.They like applying holistic techniques to therapy and may connect with people.

Environmental or Sustainability Work: Because of their inherent humanitarian inclination and desire to create positive change, 9 persons may excel in environmental or sustainability work. They enjoy promoting sustainable practises and make a positive difference in the world.

Those with Life path 9 flourish in occupations and businesses that allow them to help others, promote social justice, and express their creativity.

Master Numbers

Other life path numbers consider 11/2 and 22/4 to be powerful as they possess unique characteristics that separate them. We believe master numbers have higher spiritual purpose and a strong sense of intuition and insight. Individuals with a master life path number may experience challenges and difficulties in their lives, but they also have the potential for great success and accomplishment. We often see those with a master life path as natural leaders, healers, visionaries, and they inspire others and make a positive impact in the world.

They belong to advanced souls—people who have already mastered the simple lessons in previous incarnations and are now ready to study some of the more difficult lessons. (Someone believed reincarnation in the East.) It has reincarnated people with a master number life path numerous times and now make their mark on the world. Unfortunately, many people on the master number route find it too tough to manage and only reach a fraction of their full potential.

11/2 Life Path

The word idealism describes the 11/2 life path.

Individuals with the life path number 11 are idealistic. They are frequently visionaries; they have access to novel ideas and prefer to fantasise rather than act. They are, nonetheless, incredibly capable of whatever they do with enough determination and achieve anything. Because their ideas are not always realistic, they must carefully assess them before pursuing them. Elevens are always perceptive and thoughtful.

They are known for their abilities to motivate and inspire others. While this may be difficult for some due to their reluctance to draw attention to themselves, it is vital for them to set aside their own reservations if they are to reach their genuine goal.

They have the potential to become great artists, professors, musicians, actors, idealists, inspired, innovative, and religious leaders.

People who use the negative side of their 11 life path are unrealistic dreamers who achieve nothing and live in a world where it is difficult to distinguish between fact and fiction.

CAREER AND BUSINESS

Life path 11 is a master number that represents spiritual awakening, intuition, creativity, and leadership. Individuals that follow this path are frequently highly perceptive, have a natural capacity to understand and analyse complex situations. Here are some of the top profession and business opportunities for those with Life path 11:

Healer, Spiritual or Holistic: Careers in spiritual or holistic healing be a good fit for them due to their innate intuition and spiritual awareness. They appreciate assisting people and use their intuition to direct their work.

Careers in teaching or mentoring be a good fit for 11 people due to their natural leadership and insight. They appreciate passing on their knowledge and are capable of inspiring and guiding others.

Writer or Artist: Because of their innate inventiveness and intuition, 11 people are well-suited to occupations in writing or art. They like to express themselves and produce masterpieces that inspire others.

Entrepreneur or Business Owner: Because of their inherent leadership and insight, life path 11 individuals may excel in entrepreneurship or business owning. They enjoy taking risks and recognise opportunities that others do not.

Psychologist or Counsellor: Because of their inherent insight and empathy, they may excel in occupations in psychology or counselling. They appreciate assisting others and connect with people on an emotional level.

Philosopher or Theologian: Because of their innate spiritual sensitivity and deep thought, 11 may excel in vocations in philosophy or theology. They appreciate delving into complex issues and see the big picture.

Those with Life path 11 succeed in jobs and businesses that need intuition, creativity and leadership. They have a natural gift for spiritual awareness, sensitivity, profound thought, as they may inspire and encourage others to reach their full potential.

22/4 Life Path

Master-builder best describes the 22/4 life path.

People with the life path number 22 may do anything they set their minds. Typically, their purpose is broad in scope. They have a lot of talent that they need to harness constructively. Elevens are often dreamers; twenty-twos have dreams but make them a reality. These individuals are practical, often unconventional, and frequently charismatic. They may excite and motivate others by their words and deeds.

Those with this Destiny Number are called to participate in projects and pursuits that will benefit society as a whole. This is accomplished by implementing spiritual ideas in the material world.

22's path meaning is extremely effective. People born on this number posses a greater spiritual awareness than other master numbers. 22 also suggests a heightened ability to apply your spiritual understanding to practical objectives, which is why persons on this Life Path are frequently successful in both their spiritual and practical endeavours. They are detail-oriented, high achievers, and powerful.

CAREER AND BUSINESS

Life Path 22/4 is a master number that combines the attributes of the numbers 2 and 4. Individuals who follow this life path are thought to have a high potential for success and achievement, as well as the capacity to put their objectives and ideas into action. Here are some of the top profession and business opportunities for them: Those with the number 22/4 have a natural talent for entrepreneurship and business ownership. They understand the big picture and have the practical ability to make their ideas a reality.

Engineer or Architect: Because of their practical and logical brains, these 22/4 individuals may excel in engineering or architectural occupations. They appreciate problem solving and apply their technical knowledge in real-world circumstances.

Project Manager: Because of their capacity to see the big picture while managing minutiae, individuals with life path 22/4 may excel in project management employment. They may lead teams and ensure projects are finished on schedule and on budget.

Financial Advisor: With their practical and analytical minds, as they could excel in finance occupations. They analyse financial data and give solid advise to clients.

Philanthropist or Social Entrepreneur: 22/4 people frequently have a strong feeling of social duty and a desire to make a difference in the world. Jobs in charity or social entrepreneurship may be a good fit for them because they put their practical abilities to good use.

Individuals with life path 22/4 thrive in occupations and businesses that require practical problem-solving, leadership, and entrepreneurship. They have a natural flair for bringing their ideas to life and are capable of achieving long-term success and achievement.

Chapter 11

Name Numerology

In Chaldean name numerology, we assign each letter a specific number value based on its sound vibration. These values range from 1 to 8.

A name numerologist analyses the numerical values of a person's name to offer insights into their strengths, weaknesses, and potential for success. Name numerology select a name for a newborn, choose a new name for oneself or a business, personal growth and self-awareness. With knowledge of the Chaldean chart, letters, and specific number associations, one understand and apply name numerology.

To decide an individual's numerological value, we use their full name, as the letters in their name hold specific vibrations. The process assigns each letter in the name a numerical value based on the above table, and then adds these values together to create a single-digit number, or a master number.

One of the most common uses of this technique is to transform a person's birth name into a number.

Each part of a person's name contains unique information about them. A person's first or birth name, according to numerology standards, gives information about that person's physical condition and mental acuity. It also help us determine how that individual will act in a certain set of circumstances and how they would perceive their life experiences.

A person's middle name provides information about the emotional parts of their life and reveal a lot about their interests and fitness for marriage.

A person's surname - or family - name reveals information about their strengths and shortcomings.

1	2	3	4	5	6	7	8
A	B	C	D	E	U	O	F
I	K	G	M	H	V	Z	P
J	R	L	T	N	W		
Q		S		X			
Y							

Chaldean Numerology Chart

In this example we would examine the name:

CHALDEAN NUMEROLOGY

C	H	A	L	D	E	A	N
3	5	1	3	4	5	1	5

N	U	M	E	R	O	L	O	G	Y
5	6	4	5	2	7	3	7	3	1

STEP 1		
FIRST NAME	REDUCING	DIGIT
35134515	3 + 5 + 1 + 3 + 4 + 5 + 1 + 5	27
		9

STEP 2		
LAST NAME	REDUCING	DIGIT
5645273731	5 + 6 + 4 + 5 + 2 + 7 + 3 + 7 + 3 + 1	43
		7

STEP 3		
DIGITS	REDUCING	DIGIT
9, 7	9 + 7	16
		7

Once we assign number to each letter to First name, Middle name, and Last name we need to add all the digits and further reducing to a single digit.

7 IS NUMEROLOGY NUMBER FOR NAME: CHALDEAN NUMEROLOGY.

First Name + Last Name = 9 + 7 = 16 = 7

When summing the values of the letters in a name, unless you arrive at a master number, reduce two-digit numbers to a value of 1 through 9.

1: Beginning, autonomy, invention, leadership, and the masculine principle.

2: Harmony, togetherness, connections, teamwork, and the feminine principle.

3: Speaking one's mind, imagination, optimism, playfulness, and creativity.

4: Construction, formation, hard effort, endurance, earnestness, and practicability.

5: Change, transition, innovative thinking, resourcefulness, liberty, adaptability, and advancement.

6: Balance, nurturing, service orientation, responsibility, duty, family focus, number of marriages and divorces, home and work concerns.

7: Research, science, technology, isolation, wisdom, spiritual concentration, investigative, mystical, and metaphysical.

8: Authority, power, money, commerce, success, material worth, organisation, and self-mastery are all aspects of authority.

9: Endings, vision, tolerance, transformation, spiritual consciousness, cosmos, teaching, global awareness, and perfection are all aspects of spiritual consciousness.

11/2: Big ideas, intuitive, capable, spiritual abilities, and emotional.

22/4: master builder, faces major difficulties, capable, physical exhaustion.

Name numerology help individuals gain self-awareness, choose the right name for themselves or their business, improve relationships, and gain clarity on their life's purpose. With its numerous benefits, advantages, name numerology is a powerful tool for personal and professional growth and success.

- Self-awareness and personal growth

- Choosing the right name

- Improved relationships

- Business success

- Life path and purpose

First Name Analysis : CHALDEAN 35134515

DIGIT'S COUNT	
Number of 1s	2
Number of 2s	0
Number of 3s	2
Number of 4s	1
Number of 5s	3
Number of 6s	0
Number of 7s	0
Number of 8s	0
Number of 9s	0

One of the first things that stands out about this name is that it has three 5s, implying that the person who bears it appreciates freedom and accepts change.

Last name Analysis: NUMEROLOGY 5645273731

The presence of two 7s, as well as a last name total of 7, tells us that this person is truth seeker, research oriented with strong analytical abilities.

The presence of two 3s, as well as a first name total of 9, indicates that this person has exceptional humanitarian expressive analytical capacity.

DIGIT'S COUNT	
Number of 1s	1
Number of 2s	1
Number of 3s	2
Number of 4s	1
Number of 5s	2
Number of 6s	1
Number of 7s	2
Number of 8s	0
Number of 9s	0

Growth Numbers

Refers to the first name single digit.

1: Progress and growth can be seen in self-expression and creativity.

2: Growth and improvement are visible in connections with others.

3: Creativity appears to be a source of growth and advancement.

4: Fear and security are manifestations of growth and progress.

5: The correct use of freedom reveals growth and progress.

6: In situations of love, there is growth and advancement.

7: There appears to be mystical, spiritual insight in the growth and advancement.

8: Progress, expansion can be seen in the management of money and power.

9: Compassion, forgiveness demonstrate growth and progress.

11: Development, progress are visible through imparting spiritual truth and harmonising energy.

22: Development, progress can be seen in intuition and the application of universal principles.

Chapter 12

Compatibility

Numerology number compatibility is the practice of analysing the compatibility between two individuals based on their numerological values. Every number holds a specific vibration and energy, hence used to determine an individual's personality traits, tendencies, and life path.

NUMBERS	FRIENDS	NEUTRAL	EMENY
1	2 3 4 5 6 9	1 6 7	8
2	1 2 3 5 7	4 9	6 8
3	1 2 3 5 9	4 7 8	4 6
4	1 5 6 7	2 3 4 8	2 9
5	1 2 4 5 6 8	3 7 9	
6	4 5 6 8	1 2 3 6 7	2 9
7	4 5 6 8	1 2 3 7 9	
8	5 6 7	2 3 4 8 9	1 9
9	1 3 5 7	2 9	4 6 8 9

Certain numbers are compatible with each other, while

others may conflict or be incompatible.Numerology number compatibility helps individuals gain insight into various aspects of their relationships, such as compatibility, communication, and emotional bonding.

By understanding each other's numerological values and energies, individuals build stronger, more fulfilling relationships and work towards achieving their shared goals and aspirations. Every human being has an aura (the energy field), which harmonises their emotions, ideas, and bodies. It was those who discovered the aura balancing key who became prosperous, had better relationships, and were happier in their lives. We refer this to as the allies, neutrals, and adversaries chart in numerology. You use this chart for any situation of your life, whether you are looking for a new career, business, or relationship.

Balance and expand your aura to attract anything in your life. An aura surrounds everything on this earth,, and when you are in resonance, everything benefits you.

Think in terms of energy, frequency, and vibration if you wish to discover the secrets of the universe - Nikola Tesla.

In the globe, there are both friends and foes. It is up to you to locate them and alter your strategy. Both are present, but it is up to you to distinguish between your allies and enemies. Acquiring new friends is simple, but recognising your actual adversaries is challenging.

Did you know numbers be both your best friend and your worst enemy for numerology? You have complete discretion over how you learn your friendly and enemy numbers in the same reference, a neutral number neither your buddy nor your foe.

Your existence revolves around your birthdate, bank account number, company name, brand name, and the names of your partners.

The same context also shows a person's name, such as the total of your first, middle, and surname letters.

• 1 and 2 are compatible with each other as they balance each other.

• 2 and 7 are compatible with each other, as they share a deep understanding of each other's emotional needs.

• 3 and 5 are compatible with each other, as they are both adventurous and creative.

• 4 and 8 are compatible with each other, as they share a practical and business-oriented approach to life.

1's compatibility

In the below table we would add other positions with respect to number, planet in the celestial kingdom. The number One (1), planet SUN the KING's compatibility.

NUMBER	PLANET	POSITION	NUMBER	PLANET	POSITION	AFFINITY
1	SUN	KING	1	SUN	KING	NUTRAL
1	SUN	KING	2	MOON	QUEEN	FRIEND
1	SUN	KING	3	JUPITER	TEACHER	FRIEND
1	SUN	KING	4	RAHU	SHADOW	FRIEND
1	SUN	KING	5	MERCURY	PRINCE PRINCES	FRIEND
1	SUN	KING	6	VENUS	ASURAS TEACHER	NUTRAL
1	SUN	KING	7	KETU	SHADOW	NUTRAL
1	SUN	KING	8	SATURN	JUDGE	ENEMY
1	SUN	KING	9	MARS	COMMANDER	FRIEND

2's compatibility

The number Two (2), planet MOON the QUEEN's compatibility with respect to other position within the celestial kingdom.

NUMBER	PLANET	POSITION	NUMBER	PLANET	POSITION	AFFINITY
2	MOON	QUEEN	1	SUN	KING	FRIEND
2	MOON	QUEEN	2	MOON	QUEEN	FRIEND
2	MOON	QUEEN	3	JUPITER	TEACHER	FRIEND
2	MOON	QUEEN	4	RAHU	SHADOW	NUTRAL
2	MOON	QUEEN	5	MERCURY	PRINCE PRINCES	FRIEND
2	MOON	QUEEN	6	VENUS	ASURAS TEACHER	ENEMY
2	MOON	QUEEN	7	KETU	SHADOW	FRIEND
2	MOON	QUEEN	8	SATURN	JUDGE	ENEMY
2	MOON	QUEEN	9	MARS	COMMANDER	NUTRAL

3's compatibility

The number Three (3), planet JUPITER the Guru's compatibility with respect to other position within the celestial kingdom.

NUMBER	PLANET	POSITION	NUMBER	PLANET	POSITION	AFFINITY
3	JUPITER	TEACHER	1	SUN	KING	FRIEND
3	JUPITER	TEACHER	2	MOON	QUEEN	FRIEND
3	JUPITER	TEACHER	3	JUPITER	TEACHER	FRIEND
3	JUPITER	TEACHER	4	RAHU	SHADOW	NUTRAL ENEMY
3	JUPITER	TEACHER	5	MERCURY	PRINCE PRINCES	FRIEND
3	JUPITER	TEACHER	6	VENUS	ASURAS TEACHER	ENEMY
3	JUPITER	TEACHER	7	KETU	SHADOW	NUTRAL
3	JUPITER	TEACHER	8	SATURN	JUDGE	NUTRAL
3	JUPITER	TEACHER	9	MARS	COMMANDER	FRIEND

4's compatibility

The number Four (4), planet RAHU's compatibility with respect to other planets and number.

NUMBER	PLANET	POSITION	NUMBER	PLANET	POSITION	AFFINITY
4	RAHU	SHADOW	1	SUN	KING	FRIEND
4	RAHU	SHADOW	2	MOON	QUEEN	NUTRAL ENEMY
4	RAHU	SHADOW	3	JUPITER	TEACHER	NUTRAL
4	RAHU	SHADOW	4	RAHU	SHADOW	NUTRAL ENEMY
4	RAHU	SHADOW	5	MERCURY	PRINCE PRINCES	FRIEND
4	RAHU	SHADOW	6	VENUS	ASURAS TEACHER	FRIEND
4	RAHU	SHADOW	7	KETU	SHADOW	FRIEND
4	RAHU	SHADOW	8	SATURN	JUDGE	NUTRAL ENEMY
4	RAHU	SHADOW	9	MARS	COMMANDER	ENEMY

5's compatibility

The number Five (5), planet MERCURY the celestial princes's compatibility with respect to other position within the celestial kingdom.

NUMBER	PLANET	POSITION	NUMBER	PLANET	POSITION	AFFINITY
5	MERCURY	PRINCE PRINCES	1	SUN	KING	FRIEND
5	MERCURY	PRINCE PRINCES	2	MOON	QUEEN	FRIEND
5	MERCURY	PRINCE PRINCES	3	JUPITER	TEACHER	NUTRAL
5	MERCURY	PRINCE PRINCES	4	RAHU	SHADOW	FRIEND
5	MERCURY	PRINCE PRINCES	5	MERCURY	PRINCE PRINCES	FRIEND
5	MERCURY	PRINCE PRINCES	6	VENUS	ASURAS TEACHER	FRIEND
5	MERCURY	PRINCE PRINCES	7	KETU	SHADOW	NUTRAL
5	MERCURY	PRINCE PRINCES	8	SATURN	JUDGE	FRIEND
5	MERCURY	PRINCE PRINCES	9	MARS	COMMANDER	NUTRAL

6's compatibility

The number Six (6), planet VENUS the Asuras Guru's compatibility with respect to other position within the celestial kingdom.

NUMBER	PLANET	POSITION	NUMBER	PLANET	POSITION	FRIEND / NUTRAL / ENEMY
6	VENUS	DEVIL TEACHER	1	SUN	KING	NUTRAL
6	VENUS	DEVIL TEACHER	2	MOON	QUEEN	NUTRAL ENEMY
6	VENUS	DEVIL TEACHER	3	JUPITER	TEACHER	NUTRAL ENEMY
6	VENUS	DEVIL TEACHER	4	RAHU	SHADOW	FRIEND
6	VENUS	DEVIL TEACHER	5	MERCURY	PRINCE PRINCES	FRIEND
6	VENUS	DEVIL TEACHER	6	VENUS	ASURAS TEACHER	FRIEND
6	VENUS	DEVIL TEACHER	7	KETU	SHADOW	FRIEND
6	VENUS	DEVIL TEACHER	8	SATURN	JUDGE	FRIEND
6	VENUS	DEVIL TEACHER	9	MARS	COMMANDER	ENEMY

7's compatibility

The number Seven (7), planet KETU's compatibility with respect to other planets and number.

NUMBER	PLANET	POSITION	NUMBER	PLANET	POSITION	FRIEND / NUTRAL / ENEMY
7	KETU	SHADOW	1	SUN	KING	NUTRAL
7	KETU	SHADOW	2	MOON	QUEEN	NUTRAL
7	KETU	SHADOW	3	JUPITER	TEACHER	NUTRAL
7	KETU	SHADOW	4	RAHU	SHADOW	FRIEND
7	KETU	SHADOW	5	MERCURY	PRINCE PRINCES	FRIEND
7	KETU	SHADOW	6	VENUS	ASURAS TEACHER	FRIEND
7	KETU	SHADOW	7	KETU	SHADOW	NUTRAL
7	KETU	SHADOW	8	SATURN	JUDGE	FRIEND
7	KETU	SHADOW	9	MARS	COMMANDER	NUTRAL

8's compatibility

The number Eight (8), planet SATURN's compatibility with respect to other planets and number.

NUMBER	PLANET	POSITION	NUMBER	PLANET	POSITION	FRIEND / NUTRAL / ENEMY
8	SATURN	JUDGE	1	SUN	KING	ENEMY
8	SATURN	JUDGE	2	MOON	QUEEN	NUTRAL
8	SATURN	JUDGE	3	JUPITER	TEACHER	NUTRAL
8	SATURN	JUDGE	4	RAHU	SHADOW	NUTRAL ENEMY
8	SATURN	JUDGE	5	MERCURY	PRINCE PRINCES	FRIEND
8	SATURN	JUDGE	6	VENUS	ASURAS TEACHER	FRIEND
8	SATURN	JUDGE	7	KETU	SHADOW	FRIEND
8	SATURN	JUDGE	8	SATURN	JUDGE	NUTRAL ENEMY
8	SATURN	JUDGE	9	MARS	COMMANDER	NUTRAL ENEMY

9's compatibility

The number Nine (9), planet MARS's compatibility with respect to other planets and number.

NUMBER	PLANET	POSITION	NUMBER	PLANET	POSITION	FRIEND / NUTRAL / ENEMY
9	MARS	COMMANDER	1	SUN	KING	FRIEND
9	MARS	COMMANDER	2	MOON	QUEEN	NUTRAL
9	MARS	COMMANDER	3	JUPITER	TEACHER	FRIEND
9	MARS	COMMANDER	4	RAHU	SHADOW	ENEMY
9	MARS	COMMANDER	5	MERCURY	PRINCE PRINCES	FRIEND
9	MARS	COMMANDER	6	VENUS	ASURAS TEACHER	NUTRAL EMENY
9	MARS	COMMANDER	7	KETU	SHADOW	FRIEND
9	MARS	COMMANDER	8	SATURN	JUDGE	ENEMY
9	MARS	COMMANDER	9	MARS	COMMANDER	NUTRAL EMENY

For knowing the personality of a person, the friendship notion is helpful with numerology.

In Numerology, everyone has their own Life Path number, based on their unique birth date. The number reflects the energy that determines who we are and where we are going.

While a person's numerology chart contains many numbers, the Life Path number is the most important. It is the most important number in numerology compatibility because it exposes how we think, act and react, emotions, and interact with others.

A compatibility between the day of birth, life path, and name numerology balances and strengthens an individual's aura, produces energy, and resonates with the greater purpose in life, bringing advancement of prosperity, success, and wealth, and keeps the individual with good health in nature's harmony.

Numbers provide insight into different aspects of a relationship. A person's compatibility not be determined based on their birth number, as relationships are complex. Rather than providing a definitive answer, we should use numerology number compatibility as a tool for understanding and managing relationships.

Chapter 13

Lo Shu Grid

The first of China's five mythological emperors Wu-of-Hsia, was working on the Hwang Ho(Yellow) River 4,000 years ago, seeking to discover a means to prevent the floods that decimated the settlements along the lower and middle tributaries of the river.

While performing his tasks, Wu discovered a tortoise shell. The people believed God lived in turtle shells.

But, the markings on this tortoise shell were amazing. On the back of the turtle, Wu and his colleagues found a flawless, three-by-three magic square. The Lo Shu grid is the name of this square.

The Lo Shu Grid, also known as the Nine-Square Grid or the Magic Square, is a 3x3 grid that is central forms of Chinese divination, including Feng Shui and Nine Star Ki. They arranged the numbers in the Lo Shu Grid in a specific pattern, with each row, column, and diagonal adding up to the number 15.

It was perfect, as this discovery thrilled Wu and his advisers. Wu's successful resolution of the flooding issues earned him the title of emperor, but his real claim to fame was the discovery of this tortoise shell.

Before we understand the Lo shu Magic Grid, and its importance in life's prediction, we must attempt to memorise the below table:

3 X 3 Lo Shu Magic Grid

SE	S			SW
E	4	9	2	W
	3	5	7	
	8	1	6	
NE	N			NW

Wu's three by three magic square revealed interesting facts.

There are 3 rows, 3 columns, and 9 squares in total. Each row and column has clever names that show a variety of factors.

The top row has the digits 4, 9, and 2. The Lo Shu grid terms this row as the head, the Mental Plane. Intellectual pursuits, logical thinking, and the ability to analyse and solve problems are all represented by the mental plane.

The middle row composed the digits 3, 5, and 7, known as the Emotional Plane or body of an individual. The emotional plane is feelings, emotions, and intuition.

The bottom row has the numbers 8, 1, and 6, which represent a person's legs and feet, referred to as the practical plane. The practical plane is physical activity, practicality, and the ability to get things done.

Top row is called the Intellectual Plane. We know the middle row as the Spiritual Plane and the bot- tom row is the Material Plane.

But, for simplicity, easier reading and memorising the 3 rows we refer them as Mental, Emotional and Practical planes.

<table>
<tr><td>

MENTAL PLANE (HEAD)

EMOTIONAL PLANE (BODY)

PRACTICAL PLANE (LEGS AND FEET)

</td></tr>
</table>

Besides 3 rows, there are three columns, and each one represents different aspects.

The Left -hand column, the first vertical row composed 4, 3, and 8, called the Thought plane. The thought plane represents the power of the mind and the ability to think differently. In the Lo Shu Grid, the number 4 is associated with the thought plane, as it represents mental agility and flexibility.

Will Plane is the number 9, 5, and 1 found in the middle column. The will plane represents determination, self-discipline, and the ability to stay focused on a goal.

The Right-hand column, the last vertical row, shows numbers 2, 7, and 6, termed as Action Plane. The action plane represents physical activity, practical skills, and the ability to get things done. In the Lo Shu Grid, the number 6 is associated with the action plane, as it represents harmony and balance. People with a strong action plane are often very productive and have a talent for getting things done. They excel in fields that require physical activity and practical skills, such as construction, engineering, and manufacturing.

Top Left column also known as the Thought Plane, the middle column as Activity Plane and the right column as Strength Plane.

However, for simplicity, easier reading and memorising the 3 columns we refer them as Thought, Will and Action planes.

Mental Plane (4, 9, 2)

SE	S			SW
E	4	9	2	W
	3	5	7	
	8	1	6	
NE	N			NW

The number 4, 9, and 2 govern the Mental Plane, and these three numbers show academic potential and a superb memory. This arrow represents those who possess analytical, verbal, and logical skills but who think highly of themselves.

The number 4 is associated with the element of wood, representing growth and creativity. The number 9 is associated with the element of fire, representing transformation and passion. The number 2 is associated with the element of earth, representing stability and groundedness. Together, we believe these numbers balance growth, transformation, and stability, allowing the mind to access higher knowledge and wisdom.

Emotional Plane (3, 5, 7)

SE	S			SW
	4	9	2	
E	3	5	7	W
	8	1	6	
NE	N			NW

The numbers 3, 5, and 7 are in the Emotional Plane, the middle row. It places a strong emphasis on the spirituality, feelings, emotions, and emotional elements of each individual who possesses it.

The emotional plane depicts consciousness that exists beyond the physical plane. Growth and movement is associated with the number 3. Balance and harmony are associated with the number 5. Completion and fulfilment is associated with the number 7. People believe these numbers balance growth, harmony, and fulfilment, allowing for emotional intelligence and intuition to flourish.

Practical Plane (8, 1, 6)

SE	S			SW
E	4	9	2	W
	3	5	7	
	8	1	6	
NE	N			NW

8, 1, and 6 considered as Practical Plane, which stresses how physically fit, practical, and successful an individual is in the business and commercial spheres.

Money, career, and daily tasks are some of the material aspects of life that the practical plane is concerned with. Abundance and prosperity are associated with the number 8. Flow and flexibility are associated with the number 1 and it is associated with the element of water. The number 6 is associated with the element of metal and represents efficiency and organisation. We believe that these numbers together balance abundance, flow, and efficiency, allowing for practical and grounded action in the world.

Thought Plane (4, 3, 8)

SE	S			SW
	4	9	2	
E	3	5	7	W
	8	1	6	
NE	N			NW

The first vertical row from the left, is the Thought Plane, contains the numbers 4, 3, and 8. It defines consciousness, that is concerned with the power of thought and manifestation of ideas. Growth and creativity are associated with the number 4. The number 3 is associated with the element of fire and represents transformation and inspiration. The number 8 is associated with the element of earth and represents stability and manifestation. These numbers together balance growth, transformation, and manifestation.

It encourages individuals to focus their thoughts on positive outcomes and to take inspired action towards their goals, knowing that their thoughts have the power to manifest their reality.

Will Plane (9, 5, 1)

SE	S			SW
	4	9	2	
E	3	5	7	W
	8	1	6	
NE	N			NW

The numerals 9, 5, and 1 are in the middle known as Will Plane, emphasising the individuals' drive and motivation. The Will I believe the plane to be a realm of consciousness that is concerned with the power of will and determination? The number 9 is associated with the element of fire and represents transformation and passion. The number 5 is associated with the element of earth and represents stability and grounding. Flow and flexibility are associated with the number 1 and it is associated with the element of water. People believe these numbers balance transformation, stability, and flow, allowing for the power of will to be expressed in the world. It encourages individuals to tap into their inner strength and determination, knowing that they have the power to overcome any obstacle and achieve their goals.

Action Plane (2, 7, 6)

SE	S			SW
E	4	9	2	W
	3	5	7	
	8	1	6	
NE	N			NW

The vertical row on the right, known as the Action Plane, takes up positions 2, 7, and 6. We believe the Action Plane to be a realm of consciousness that is concerned with the power of action and manifestation in the world. The number 2 is associated with the element of earth and represents stability and balance. The number 6, and 7 is associated with the element of metal and represent efficiency and organisation. People believe these numbers balance stability, efficiency, and transformation together, allowing for the power of action to be expressed in the world.

It encourages individuals to take practical steps towards their desired outcomes, knowing that their actions have the power to manifest their reality. Proceed to preparing, reading, and analysing individual's chart, and place the required numbers across Mental, Emotional, Practical, Thought, Will and Action planes.

Aside from the aforementioned planes, there are also arrows. An arrow joins diagonal numbers and contains two or three numbers, so it represent a variety of qualities of a person. The Arrows of Strength are said to provide guidance and inspiration for those seeking to cultivate inner strength and personal power, reminding us to tap into powerful energies and resources within ourselves to achieve our goals and overcome obstacles.

Arrows:

- The golden arrow (4,5,6)

- The silver arrow (2,5,8)

- The Detail Arrow (1,3)

- The Litigation Arrow (3, 9)

- The Peace Arrow (7, 9)

- The Science, and Technology Arrow (1, 7)

3 Number's arrows

The Golden arrow is present when a person's chart has numbers 4,5 and 6.

The Silver arrow is formed when a person's chart shows numbers 2, 5 and 8.

Both Golden and Silver Arrow represents success.

- The Golden Arrow (4, 5, 6)

- The Silver Arrow (2, 5, 8)

SE	S			SW
E	4	9	2	W
	3	5	7	
	8	1	6	
Silver Arrow	N		Golden Arrow	

The Golden arrow (4, 5, 6)

SE	S			SW
	4	9	2	
E	3	5	7	W
	8	1	6	
NE	N			NW

The 4-5-6 arrow is a powerful symbol that connects the planes of practicality, emotions, and mental faculties. The 4-5-6 arrow represents the flow of energy between these three planes, suggesting that success and material stability be achieved through the harmonious balance of practicality, emotions, and mental faculties.

This arrow urges us to use our inner wisdom and intuition to make practical and emotionally rewarding decisions, as well as to use our mental faculties to strategies and plan for success. We gain a greater sense of balance and fulfilment in our lives by understanding the interplay of these three planes and attempting to harmonise them.

The Silver arrow (2, 5, 8)

SE	S			SW
E	4	9	2	W
	3	5	7	
	8	1	6	
NE	N			NW

This arrow represents the interplay between these three planes and the flow of energy that connects them. The 2-5-8 arrow represents the flow of energy between these three planes, suggesting that material success and abundance be achieved through the harmonious balance of action, emotions, and practicality. This arrow encourages us to tap into our inner wisdom and intuition to make decisions that align with our values and passions, and to use our practical skills to manifest our goals in the material world. By understanding the interplay of these three planes and working to harmonise them, we achieve greater success and abundance in our lives.

2 Number's arrows

- ❧ The Detail Arrow (1,3)

- ❧ The Litigation Arrow (3, 9)

- ❧ The Peace Arrow (7, 9)

- ❧ The Science, and Technology Arrow (1, 7)

The Detail Arrow (1, 3)

SE	S			SW
E	4	9	2	W
	3	5	7	
	8	1	6	
NE	N			NW

When 1, and 3 are present in a chart, the Detail Arrow is formed. This means that everything is covered in detail, described and executed perfectly. The 3-1 arrow is a powerful symbol that connects the emotion, and willpower planes.

The Litigation Arrow (3, 9)

SE	S			SW
	4	9	2	
E	3	5	7	W
	8	1	6	
NE	N			NW

The Litigation Arrow is generated when the numbers 3 and 9 are present in a chart. They might encounter disputes and disagreements. When encountering the 3,9 arrow, individuals are encouraged to focus on their goals and to trust in the power of the universe to guide them towards success. This symbol is said to represent upward momentum, progress, and positive change, making it an encouraging sign for those seeking to make positive changes in their lives.

The Peace Arrow (7, 9)

SE	S			SW
E	4	9	2	W
	3	5	7	
	8	1	6	
NE	N			NW

The Peace Arrow is produced when the numbers 7 and 9 are present in a chart. They discover peace in many situations, explore spiritualism, and are upbeat, self-assured, and religious.

The rationalism of the 9 supports the spirituality of the 7, and vice versa. These people are able to handle challenging circumstances with composure and faith that everything will turn out for the best.

The Science, and Technology Arrow (1, 7)

SE	S			SW
E	4	9	2	W
	3	5	7	
	8	1	6	
NE	N			NW

The Science identified when the numbers 1 and 7 present. They are persistent, explorative, and interested in the mysteries of our world. They adore discovering hidden truths and sometimes become so engrossed in their studies that they lose track of time. This arrow acquired its name because they are typically interested in the sciences, frequently those that relate to the oceans.

*** The Lo Shu grid pattern has an outer border where the odd and even numbers alternate; the four even numbers are at the corners, and the five odd numbers, which outweigh the even numbers by one, create a cross in the middle.

Numbers Significance

Number 1: Independence, leadership, creativity

On the material plane, one is in the centre. It is regarded as a favourable number since it denotes a person who has the capacity to earn money and lead a fulfilling life.

Financially, those with a 1 in the chart will be okay. If the other two numbers on the material plane, 8 and 6, are present, the likelihood of financial success increases signifitly, forming the arrow of prosperity.

Financial success is guaranteed for those having the number two in their birth chart. They also have a tendency to be fortunate. In addition to the arrow of wealth, the presence of two or three 7s in the chart indicates that the subject is exceptionally adaptable and capable of tremendous success in a variety of fields.

Number 2: Partnership, balance, harmony

On the Mental Plane, number 2 is located in the upper right-hand corner. The fact that it appears so frequently makes it the least fortunate number for the intellect. The number two is considered a neutral or negative number unless it appears with the numbers 4 and 9, which together form the arrow of the mind.

Two 2s alone result in a loss of vitality and the possibility of sickness. However, the meaning is considerably more uplifting when the two 2s are found as a component of the arrows of the intelligence or willpower. As a result, the person's mental abilities are improved, and they have a good, clear mind and an amazing memory.

Unless they are bolstered by the arrows of intelligence or tenacity, three 2s are seen to be particularly unfortunate. The presence of three consecutive 2s is a sign of severe sickness.

Number 3: Expression, communication, creativity

The middle row of the where you'll find the number 3, which is the first of the spiritual numbers.

People with a 3 in their chart require the support of either the numbers 8 and 4 or 5 and 7 (forming the emotional arrow) (creating the Though arrow) People with one 3 are easily harmed and experience tension if one or both of these numbers are missing.

A person will develop a strong faith and way of life if the two 3s are a part of their spiritual arrow.

Those who have three 3s are oversensitive. Because they live in an illusory dream world of their own making, they are constantly harmed by their concern for spirituality, sensitivity, and intuition.

Number 4: Stability, foundation, order

Four is an intriguing number. This is so because in some Chinese dialects, the number four has a similar sound to the word death. As a result, it's commonly thought of as a negative number. However, it could be advantageous in some situations. 3 People with high intelligence have the number 4, which is located in the top left square of the Mental Plane in Eastern numerology.

The number four is associated with sensible, prudent, and intelligent people. The other numbers in the chart indicate the various fields in which these attributes be applied.

People with two 4s are more likely to be intolerant, stubborn, and self-righteous. People with two 4s have great brains and know how to use them. They should work on improving their interpersonal skills because they have a tendency to think of themselves as better than other people.

Three 4s in a chart indicate someone who is exceedingly rigid and unyielding.

Number 5: Change, adaptability, freedom

The chart's centre is occupied by the number 5. It represents a balance in Western numerology. In the East, it shows how strongly someone is feeling and feeling.

A 5 in a person's chart indicates emotional equilibrium. They make the proper choices on instinct, especially if their charts also feature the arrows of spirituality or willpower.

People with just one 5 , nevertheless, exhibit considerable character strength if the numbers 2 and 3 are absent.

Two 5s in a person's chart indicate a person who is passionate, eager, and full of life. They take pleasure in difficulties and are happiest when showcasing their ability. They have a strong sense of self-assurance and ambition. If the two 5s are a component of the arrow of willpower, these traits are strengthened (1, 5, and 9). However, if these people not find an appropriate outlet for their abilities, the two 5s could potentially be detrimental. Sometimes these people overindulge in alcohol, drugs, and sexual activity. People who have three 5s are more likely to be domineering and overbearing.

Number 6: Service, responsibility, love

The Material Plane's rightmost square contains the number 6. Due to its location on the Material Plane, it stands for material success and a comfortable way of life.

People with a 6 in their birth chart are more likely to experience minor luck. It almost certainly ensures a life free of monetary issues when it is a component of the arrow of prosperity. When it stands alone, without the digits 8 and 1, it denotes that the individual prosper financially while working in the arts.

A single 6's creative potential is frequently focused on the home. These individuals value their families and like living and working in beautiful settings. People with a single 6 frequently begin aiding less fortunate members of the community as their financial circumstances improve. This quality is highlighted more so if the number 6 is included in the action arrow.

Those who have two 6s are extremely inventive, but lack self-assurance. They overthink things, and it take them a while to bounce back from even minor losses.

These folks function best when their loved ones offer them gentle support and encouragement.

Three 6s tend to make people constantly worry about their loved ones.

Number 7: Spirituality, introspection, wisdom

In the Spiritual Plane's right-hand square, the number seven is written. As a 7 represents spirituality, intuition, and a growing faith, its appearance in the chart is a sign of good fortune. Once they approach middle age, people with a 7 in their charts become increasingly conscious of its significe.

Without the numbers 3 and 5, the number 7 in the chart stands for someone who is interested in discovering hidden truths and who strives for perfection. A single 7 with an arrow of prosperity next to it denotes a successful and compassionate individual.

The pomp and circumstance of the spiritual life tends to appeal to people with two 7s more than the spirituality itself.

Number 8: Material success, power, abundance

Because it is in the left-hand square at the beginning of the Material Plane, the number eight has a prime location in the diagram. The number 8 has always been well-liked in China since it is said to symbolise money.

The number 8 in the chart, with the digits 1 and 6, stands for effectiveness, financial stability, and careful planning. It stands for considerable financial success and a happy life when coupled with the numbers 1 and 6 to form the "arrow of prosperity." If the chart additionally shows the numbers 5 and 7, this happiness is heightened.

Business is particularly successful for those having two 8s. They typically have a very nice retirement as a result.

Number 9: Universal love, spiritual awareness, compassion

Nine is a very lucky number because it represents completion and the fusion of heaven and earth. A 9 in a chart also indicates prosperity some day in the future. This stands for idealism, altruism, and aspiration.

Those who have two 9s in their birth chart are intelligent and appreciate studying. They are thoughtful individuals who take intellectual stimulation seriously. The sole drawback of the two 9s is that they frequently only use their heads and ignore their hearts.

If you refer the 3X3 Lo shu Magic Square, you could notice the direction of each number:

- 1: North

- 2: South-West

- 3: East

- 4: South-East

- 5: Center, Balanced

- 6: North-West

- 7: West

- 8: North-East

- 9: South

In the earlier pages, we understood the numbers and its planet association. As per Loshu Grid, each number also represents an element. There are Five elements as per Chinese astrology and each number in the grid does depict an element.

Five elements

- Wood

- Fire

- Earth

- Metal

- Water

Everything on the planet could categorise using one of these elements. These elements have the capacity to be both beneficial and harmful. As a result, when creating a Loshu Grid for an individual, a consultant may discover that if any numbers or associated elements are lacking, appropriate remedies would be applied to each missing part.

Numbers and Element association:

- I relates to water

- 2 relates to earth

- 3 relates to wood

- 4 relates to wood

- 5 relates to earth

- 6 relates to metal

- 7 relates to metal

- 8 relates to earth

- 9 relates to fire

Before you plan creating an individual's Lo Shu chart, you need to fill the Loshu Grid with the following numbers. Once you fill the chart, you may wonder with repeated numbers, or missing numbers, accordingly a balanced reading with prediction, and missing number remedies need to report for the details analysis.

- Birth details (Day, Month, Year)

- First name number

- Middle, and last name number

- Personality number

- Life-path number

- Kua number

Kua number calculation

In Feng shui, kua is found in your birth year and sex. The Eight Mansions or Eight Houses of Feng Shui are other names for it. Your Kua number is used to establish the best directions to face and locations for key rooms in your house, such as your bedroom and front door. It also provides information on how well you and other people mesh energetically.

Kua number is calculated based on Male and Female with a simple formula:

For Women

- Reducing birth year into a single digit

- Example: 1979: 1 + 9 + 7 + 9 = 26

- Keep reducing to a single digit:

-     2 + 6 = 8

- Add 4 to the single-digit number

- 8 + 4 = 12

- Keep reducing 1 + 2 = 3

- Reduce to a single-digit number, if required

- Kua number = 3 for women born in 1979

For Men

- Reducing birth year into a single digit

- Example: 1976: 1 + 9 + 7 + 6 = 23

- Keep reducing to a single digit:

2 + 3 = 5

- Subtract that number from 11

  11 - 5 = 6

- Reduce to a single-digit number, if required

- Kua number = 6 for man born in 1976

We now ready to decode Subhas Chandra Bose date of birth in to Lo She magic Square.

23 January 1897

First Name: SUBHAS = 20 = 2 + 0 = 2

Middle Name: CHANDRA = 21 = 2 + 1 = 3

Last Name: BOSE = 17 = 1+7 = 8

Reducing name number: 2 + 3 + 8 = 13 = 4

Birth details:

23 January 1897

As we decoded the required numbers for Subhas Chandra Bose, born on 23 January 1897, we could plot the Loshu Grid with the derived numbers:

- Born on: 23 01 1897

- Name Number: 4

- ·❦· Personality Number: 5

- ·❦· Life-path Number: 4

- ·❦· Kua Number: 10 - 7 = 3

Life-path		
DAY	**MONTH**	**YEAR**
23	01	1897
2+3+1+1+8+9+7 = 31		
31 = 3+1 = 4		

Lo Shu Grid: Subhas Chandra Bose

SE	S			SW
E	<u>4</u> <u>4</u>	9	2	W
	3 <u>3</u>	<u>5</u>	7	
	8	11		
NE	N			NW

Chapter 14

Missing Numbers

Numerology being a predictive science, it assured remedies when someone's chart appears missing one or two numbers. If you surround yourself with items made of the element that corresponds to the missing number, it will be "treated" or fixed.

It continues to offer cures based on the colour of the planet and even the geographical direction. If only one number in a row was "cured", we could eliminate the arrow of weakness.

While plotting someone's grid let's say, we notice there is one missing number in the grid - the number 5. People say that this missing number represents a void or imbalance in the individual's life and believe it signifies challenges and obstacles on their path to success.

According to tradition, there are remedies that restore balance and harmony to the Lo Shu Grid. In this chapter, we explore a few remedies for missing numbers.

Missing 1

If someone's grid is missing the number 1, it signify a void or imbalance in their life. The number 1 represents new beginnings, independence, and leadership, and its absence   signify a lack of direction or purpose in the individual's life. Individuals use many remedies to bring balance and harmony into their life to overcome this imbalance. One solution is to concentrate on developing independence and leadership skills, as well as creating specific goals and objectives for the future. Spending time in nature, meditating, or engaging in other disciplines that aid to ground and centre the individual is one choice.

LUCKY COLOURS : Gold, Flame, Yellows and bronze to golden brown

METAL: Gold

DAY: Good deeds on Sunday

ELEMENT: Water

DIRECTION: North

REPRESENTS: Fame

1 is associated with water. Anything that is black or blue will work.

Missing 2

It signifies a void or imbalance in balance, harmony, and partnership areas. If someone is feeling imbalanced in their life, there are many remedies they   try to restore harmony. One approach is to focus on building strong relationships with others.

LUCKY COLOURS : Salmon pink, Pearl/Cream, White, Garnet, Fire, Gold,

METAL: Silver

DAY: MONDAY

ELEMENT: Earth

DIRECTION: South West

REPRESENTS: Relationships

2 is of the Earth's element number, As the three numbers 8, 5, and 2 forms the Silver arrow. You surround yourself with things that are from the ground but are not made of metal to make up for the absence of anyone or all of these numbers. The "cure" made from quartz crystals is especially effective.

Missing 3

The number 3 symbolises creativity, communication, and self-expression. Its absence suggests that the person may struggle with expressing themselves creatively or communicating effectively with others. To overcome this imbalance, there are various remedies that individuals try to bring balance and harmony into their lives. One option is to focus on developing creative skills and engaging in activities like writing, painting, or music. Another approach is to practice effective communication skills, such as active listening, empathy, and assertiveness.

LUCKY COLOURS : Rose, Ruby, Amber

METAL: Tin, Brass

DAY: Thursday

ELEMENT: Wood

DIRECTION: East

REPRESENTS: Health

Employ wooden items like furniture and ornaments. The best remedies are made of living wood since the word "tree" is commonly associated with the element wood.

Missing 4

It could indicate challenges related to stability and foundation. The number 4 is associated with the element of wood and symbolises growth and stability. Therefore, its absence may suggest difficulties in areas like financial stability, relationship stability, or stability in one's living environment.

Incorporating the number 4 into life or surroundings. For example, using wood-based decor, bringing in plants, or focusing on personal growth and development help.

COLOURS : Brown, Gray, Blue, Indigo, Silver

METAL: Copper

ELEMENT: Wood

DIRECTION: SouthEast

REPRESENTS: Wealth

Brown or greyish cloak clothes on Saturday. Keep your home and surroundings pleasant, clean and tidy. They might need to favour using wooden goods like tables, glasses, and bamboo grafts. Keep South-East landscapes lush with greenery. Donations are viewed as favourable for any charts that have missing numbers.

Missing 5

If someone's grid is missing the number 5, it may indicate challenges related to personal balance, growth, creativity, and communication. The number 5 is associated with the element of earth and represents stability, balance, and creativity.

To remedy this, one consider incorporating the number 5 in their life or surroundings, such as through the use of earth-based decor, bringing in natural materials, or focusing on creative pursuits and self-expression.

COLOURS : Green

METAL: Brass

DAY: Wednesday

ELEMENT: Earth

DIRECTION: Center

REPRESENTS: Well-Being

You surround yourself with things that are from the ground but are not metal to make up for the absence of number 5. Using quartz crystals as a "cure" is especially beneficial.

Missing 6

If the number 6 is missing from someone's Lo Shu grid, it could indicate challenges related to relationships, family, and balance. Its absence may suggest difficulties in areas like strained relationships, conflict within the family, or finding balance in life.

To address this imbalance, one try incorporating the number 6 into their life or surroundings. This be done by using metal-based decor, bringing in nurturing elements like plants, or focusing on building and strengthening relationships.

LUCKY COLOURS : White, Orange, Pink

METAL: Copper

DAY: Friday

ELEMENT: Metal

DIRECTION: North West

REPRESENTS: Helpful People

A gold or silver ring or bracelet works wonders as a "cure." Metal is also frequently referred to as gold, which essentially means money. Therefore, metal coins be viewed as a "cure."

Missing 7

If someone's grid is missing the number 7, it may indicate challenges related to spirituality, intuition, and personal growth. Thus, the absence of 7 in the Lo Shu grid may suggest difficulties in these areas, such as feeling disconnected from one's inner self, lacking spiritual guidance, or struggling to make progress in personal growth.

Incorporating number 7 into one's life or surroundings, such as by employing water-based decor, embracing practises that increase intuition and spiritual, or focusing on personal growth and development.

LUCKY COLOURS : Purple, Magenta, Blue, Indigo

METAL: Silver

ELEMENT: Metal

DIRECTION: West

REPRESENTS: Education

Since the number seven stands for the metal element, wearing a watch or bracelet with a silver chain.

They might need to dress in bright colours like white, light blue, and light green.

Missing 8

If number 8 is missing, it may signal problems with prosperity, success, and abundance. The number 8 is related with the element of earth and denotes prosperity, money, and success in numerology. Consequently, the lack of 8 indicates challenges in various areas, such as financial troubles, failure to achieve job or personal objectives, or feeling unsatisfied in life.

To address this, consider incorporating the number 8 into their life or surroundings, such as by adopting earth-based decor, focusing on wealth and abundance, or taking action to achieve financial and personal success.

LUCKY COLOURS : Blue, Grey, Black, Ivory

METAL: Iron, Platinum

DAY: Saturday

ELEMENT: Earth

DIRECTION: NorthEast

REPRESENTS: Knowledge

Wear blue or black clothing on Saturdays, keep crystals in the northeast, and surround yourself with objects that come from the earth.

Missing 9

If someone's Lo Shu grid is missing number nine, it have an impact on the results of divination. The number nine is considered a lucky number in Chinese culture, and its absence signify the absence of luck or the need to work harder to achieve success. However, missing number 9 in a Lo Shu grid does not necessarily mean bad luck or misfortune, as there are other ways to interpret the results of divination.

LUCKY COLOURS : Red, Lavender, Olive

METAL: Copper

DAY: Tuesday

ELEMENT: Fire

DIRECTION: South

REPRESENTS: Action

Wear red thread around your wrist and surround yourself with bright things, especially anything that emit light. Fire is also associated with anything red.

To help you pass for now, dress in the colour of your chart's number. It's not required to dress entirely in a single colour. If you keep in mind what it stands for and why you are using it, you use a handkerchief, a tie, an accessory, a pen or pencil in your purse, or even a piece of colourful paper in your wallet. The thought is strengthened by adding a vase or other decorative item to the house or workplace.

The colour of formal clothing is black. Although it is opulent and regal, wearing too much black symbolises sadness and loss. It draws in and isolates the feelings. It does not inspire fidelity and genuine love, nor does it stand for enduring relationships.

If you must wear black, add colour to something, even just your undergarments.

Using these colours in your home or workspace help to balance the energies of the Lo Shu grid and enhance the flow of energy in your life. You incorporate these colours through decor items, such as paintings, rugs, or pillows, or by using coloured lighting. It is important to note that these are just general guidelines and that the specific colours and colour combinations may vary based on your personal preferences and the specific Feng Shui principles that you are following.

Feng Shui Remedies

In Feng Shui, the missing numbers in the Lo Shu Grid are believed to represent specific areas of life that may be lacking or in need of attention. Here are some remedies that be used to balance the missing numbers and improve the energy flow in the associated areas:

If you have a Lo Shu grid with missing numbers, here are some remedies you try:

Missing Number 1: Place a metallic object or a statue made of metal in the affected area. You also use colours like gold, silver, or white to attract positive energy.

Missing Number 2: Use plants or wood-based items like furniture or decorative pieces to create a wood element in the affected area. The colour green is also associated with this element.

Missing Number 3: The colours red, orange, and purple are associated with this element.

Missing Number 4: Use natural stones, crystals, or ceramics to create an earth element in the affected area. The colours brown, beige, and yellow are associated with this element.

Missing Number 5: Use metal wind chimes or bells to attract positive energy. The color white is also associated with this element.

Missing Number 6: Use water-based items like fountains or aquariums to create the water element in the affected area. The colors blue and black are associated with this element.

Missing Number 7: Use mirrors or reflective surfaces to create the metal element in the affected area. The colours gold, silver, and white are associated with this element.

Missing Number 8: Use plants or wood-based items like furniture or decorative pieces to create a wood element in the affected area. The colour green is also associated with this element.

Missing Number 9: Use natural stones, crystals, or ceramics to create an earth element in the affected area. The colours brown, beige, and yellow are associated with this element.

Identify the missing number's corresponding element: Each number in the Lo Shu grid is associated with a specific element, such as water, fire, or earth. If a number is missing, you determine its corresponding element and incorporate that element into your home or workspace. For example, if the missing number is 1, which corresponds to water, you add a water feature to your home or workspace to balance the missing element.

Use a replacement number: If a number is missing from your Lo Shu grid, you try using a replacement number that has similar numerological or elemental qualities. For example, if the missing number is 5, which corresponds to earth, you use the number 8 as a replacement, which also corresponds to earth.

Place a mirror in the missing area: In Feng Shui, mirrors are often used to reflect and balance energy in a space. If there is a missing number in your Lo Shu grid, you place a mirror in the corresponding area to reflect and balance the energy of the missing number. Use Feng Shui cures: Feng Shui offers a variety of cures to balance the energy in a space, such as crystals, plants, and wind chimes.

It's important to note that these remedies are based on traditional Feng Shui principles and should be used in combination with other forms of personal growth and self-care.

Chapter 15

Numbers and Human Body

Each number corresponds to a different body part. Particularly if little thought or care has been given to the person's physical well-being, the day of the month is frequently enough to provide a clue to a fundamental bodily state.

The first number (1):

Is associated with the brain and lungs. Due to the inability to put the original ideas to use, people with several ones in the name may develop an inferiority complex, which   lead to illness. Specialised breathing exercises improve your life and are incredibly beneficial.

Two (2):

Relates to the brain, solar plexus, and neurological system. Because of its sensitivity, the physical body is quickly harmed by loud, harsh environments and coarse associations.

Three (3):

Refers to the larynx, throat, tongue, and speech organs. With many threes, illness is frequently brought on by emotional difficulties, the perception of being unpopular, issues with friendships, and self-consciousness. Less time should be spent worrying about what others might say and do spent time cultivating an optimistic outlook.

Four (4):

Relates to the top side of the body, the right arm, and the stomach. Overindulging in fatty foods results in weight gain and high blood pressure. The four's fine endurance is worn down by extended periods of intense effort. Too much seriousness in the mind result in an absence of vitality and circulation.

Five (5):

Governs the liver, gall bladder, left arm, and upper left half of the body are all represented by number five. Overactivity, restlessness, internal unhappiness, and crucial mental conditions all contribute to many fives and cause neurological tension, which disrupts the body's overall physical coordination.

Six (6):

Relates to the skin, blood, and heart. Many times, cardiac problems are biological rather than the modern-day Sudden Cardiac Arrest. These are primarily in categories four and five. Breakdowns are avoided by having a well-planned eating and living schedule. Chronic diseases caused by family issues, child infidelity, and a lack of love and acceptance.

Seven (7):

The spleen, white blood cells, and the sympathetic nervous system are all represented by number seven. All sevens require a diet and are innately picky eaters. It's crucial to take breaks from the stressful demands of public life and enjoy some peace and quiet. Repression of feelings and emotions results in poor physical health.

Eighth (8):

The colon, eyes, and lower bowels are represented by this number. Ulcers, anxious indigestion, headaches come from excessive intensity, strenuous living. The number eight has the greatest physical stamina and the best capacity for recovery. The fine body strength and endurance are maintained by maintaining an inner calm, regulated activity with outdoor sports, and regular physical activity.

Nine (9):

Relates to the kidneys and other generative organs. Additionally, high living, self-indulgence, and unhealthy habits lead to diseases that are difficult to control. Never use drugs or alcohol if your number is 9. Being healthy means avoiding being overly impressionable and living too much in your dreams and visions.

Chapter 16

Repeated Numbers

The signifies of repeated numbers varies based on the number itself, and it have both positive and negative connotations. As a result, they reveal vital information about a person's life journey and impending challenges. By assessing these data and their importance, we develop a better insight leading to enhanced personal growth and self-awareness.

Repeated numbers are not necessarily considered "bad," but seen as indicators that the individual may need to pay closer attention to their spiritual alignment and personal growth.

When a number repeated, it amplifies and associated altered energy vibration. This means that the individual may be experiencing a stronger influence from that particular number, and it may be calling their attention to a certain aspect of their life that needs more focus and attention.

However, if you feel that repeated numbers are causing negative effects in your life, here are some remedies you try:

Meditation: Regular meditation help to calm the mind and reduce stress, which in turn help to balance out the effects of repeated numbers in numerology.

Chanting mantras: Chanting mantras help to balance the energy associated with repeated numbers in numerology. For example, chanting the "Om" mantra help to balance the energy associated with the number 1.

Practice mindfulness: Repeated numbers may appear when we are not fully present or aware of our surroundings. By practicing mindfulness and being fully present in the moment, you may be able to reduce the frequency of repeated numbers.

Change your thought patterns: Negative thought patterns or limiting beliefs also contribute to the appearance of repeated numbers. By working on changing your thought patterns and focusing on positive affirmations, you may be able to shift the energy and reduce the appearance of repeated numbers.

Use gemstones: Certain gemstones, such as amethyst and clear quartz, are believed to help balance and harmonise energy. By carrying or wearing a gemstone that resonates with you, you may be able to reduce the impact of repeated numbers.

Repeated numbers have different interpretations, depending on the context and the specific numbers. Here are some general interpretations:

Repeated 1: Repeated number 1 signifies a time of transformation and change, as the number one is often associated with growth, progress, and forward movement. Therefore, seeing multiple ones in numerology indicate that the individual is on the right path and will continue to make progress toward their goals. However, it is important to note that, in some interpretations of numerology, the number 1 is also associated with arrogance and stubbornness. Therefore, if an individual sees too many ones in their numerology chart, it be a warning to balance their confidence with humility and avoid becoming too rigid in their thinking or behaviour.

Repeated 2: Repeated number 2 signifies a need for balance in all areas of life, including work, family, and personal interests. The number two is often viewed as a complement to the number one, representing the importance of collaboration and teamwork in achieving success. Therefore, if an individual sees too many twos, it be a warning to avoid becoming too dependent on others and to take more assertive action to achieving their goals.

Repeated 3: Repeated number 3 could mean a time of growth and expansion, as the number three is often associated with the concept of "trinity," representing the union of mind, body, and spirit. Therefore, seeing multiple threes in numerology indicate that the individual is entering a period of balance and harmony, where their thoughts, feelings, and actions are in alignment. However, it is important to note that, in some interpretations of numerology, the number 3 is also associated with indecision and lack of focus. Therefore, if an individual sees too many 3 in their numerology chart, it be a warning to avoid becoming scattered or unfocused and to maintain clarity and direction in their goals.

Repeated 4: Repeated number 4 signifies a time of hard work and dedication, as the number four is associated with discipline, focus, and determination. Subsequently, seeing multiple fours in numerology indicates that the individual is entering a period of intense effort and commitment, where their ability to plan, organise, and execute their goals will be crucial. Nevertheless, it is essential to be aware that, in a few understandings of numerology, the number 4 is also linked to stiffness and intransigence. Hence, if an individual notices too many fours in their numerology chart, it be a caution to evade becoming too fixed or obstinate in their thinking or behaviour.

Repeated 5: Repeated number 5 means a time of transition and transformation, as the number five is often associated with growth, progress, and evolution. Therefore, seeing multiple fives in numerology indicate that the individual is entering a period of change and transition, where their ability to adapt and navigate new challenges will be crucial. However, it is important to note that, in some interpretations of numerology, the number 5 is also associated with impulsiveness and restlessness. Therefore, if an individual sees too many fives in their numerology chart, it be a warning to avoid becoming too scattered or unfocused and to maintain clarity and direction in their goals.

Repeated 6: Repeated number 6 amplifies its qualities and indicates a need for the individual to focus on creating a harmonious and loving environment in their personal and professional life. The number 6 in numerology often signifies a time of nurturing and caring, associated with family, community, and domesticity. Thus, seeing multiple sixes in numerology may indicate that the individual is entering a period of emotional and spiritual growth, where their ability to cultivate loving relationships and support others will be crucial. However, it is important to note that some interpretations of numerology associate the number 6 with codependency and overprotectiveness. Therefore, if an individual sees too many sixes in their numerology chart, it be a warning to avoid becoming too attached or dependent on others and to maintain healthy boundaries in their relationships.

Repeated 7: Multiple 7 could amplify 7's qualities and suggest a need for the individual to focus on their spiritual and intellectual development. Repeated number 7 indicates a time of introspection and self-discovery, as the number seven is often associated with inner wisdom, self-reflection, and meditation. Therefore, seeing multiple sevens in numerology indicate that the individual is entering a period of deep introspection and exploration, where their ability to connect with their inner self and spiritual guidance will be crucial. However, it is important to note that, in some interpretations of numerology, the number 7 is also associated with isolation and detachment. Therefore, if an individual sees too many sevens in their numerology chart, it be a warning to avoid becoming too detached or withdrawn from others and to maintain healthy social connections.

Repeated 8: The repeated number 8 is considered a powerful and prosperous digit, representing abundance, success, authority, and ambition. Multiple number 8 in numerology also signify a time of personal power and achievement, as the number eight is often associated with material success, business acumen, and leadership. Therefore, seeing multiple eights in numerology indicate that the individual is entering a period of professional growth and success, where their ability to take calculated risks and make strategic decisions will be crucial. However, it is important to note that in some interpretations of numerology, the number 8 is also associated with materialism and greed. Therefore, if an individual sees too many eights in their numerology chart, it be a warning to avoid becoming too focused on material success and to maintain a balanced perspective on wealth and success.

Repeated 9: In numerology, the repeated number 9 is considered a powerful and transformative digit, representing spirituality, humanitarianism, and selflessness. When repeated in numerology, the number 9 amplify these qualities and suggest a need for the individual to focus on their spiritual and humanitarian pursuits. Repeated number 9 in numerology also signify a time of transformation and completion, as the number nine is often associated with endings, spiritual enlightenment, and service to others. Therefore, seeing multiple nines in numerology indicate that the individual is entering a period of personal growth and transformation, where their ability to let go of old patterns and embrace new perspectives will be crucial. However, it is important to note that in some interpretations of numerology, the number 9 is also associated with martyrdom and self-sacrifice. Therefore, if an individual sees too many nines in their numerology chart, it be a warning to avoid becoming too self-sacrificing and to maintain a healthy balance between serving others and caring for oneself.

Seeing recurring numbers like 111 or 222 may indicate that the individual needs to pay closer attention to their thoughts and in alignment with their higher spiritual path. Seeing 444 or 888 may indicate that the individual has to focus on their material and financial while maintaining balance.

In essence, recurring numbers in numerology serve as potent reminders to the individual that they must maintain balance and alignment in all aspects of their life, including their physical, emotional, mental, and spiritual well-being.

Chapter 17

Vedic Numerology

Vedic numerology, also known as Indian numerology or Hindu numerology, is a system of numerology that originated in ancient India. It is based on the idea that numbers have a special significe and vibrational energy that influence an individual's life path and personality.

The Vedic grid is a 3x3 square grid, the other names are Vedic/Safriel/Predictive grid.

3	1	9
6	7	5
2	8	4

Vedic numerology is used to analyse an individual's birth date and name, as well as other astrological factors, to determine their key numerological indicators. These indicators   include the individual's life path number, destiny number, and soul urge number, among others.

The interpretation of Vedic numerology is complex and multifaceted, taking into account various astrological and cultural factors. It is often used in conjunction with other forms of Vedic astrology, such as Jyotish, to provide a more comprehensive analysis of an individual's life path and potential.

In Vedic numerology chart we do not include century of a person's birth details.

23 January 1897

- Born on: 23 01 1897

- Personality number: 5

- Life-path number: 5 + 1 + 7 = 13 = 4

3	1	9
	7	<u>5</u>
2		<u>4</u>

Exception: If someone born on either 1,2, 3, 4, 5, 6, 7, 8, 9, 10, 20, or 30 then there is no need to include day of birth as its exactly same as personality number, but when personality number needed to be reduced then we add as earlier example 20 January 1897:

- Personality number: 20 = 2+0 = 2

- Life-path number: 2+1+1+8+9+7 = 28 = 1

	11	9
	7	
2		

Dasha

In vedic numerology, a dasha is a time period associated with a particular numerical vibration. Each dasha is said to influence a person's life in different ways, depending on the numerical energy associated with that dasha. There are different types of dasha in Vedic numerology, including:

1. Maha Dasha: This is the main dasha, which is associated with a person's personality number. The Maha Dasha is a long-term period, typically lasting several years, during which a person's life is influenced by the energy associated with their associated planet and the dasha number.

2. Antar Dasha: This is a sub-period within a Maha Dasha, and is associated with a specific numerical vibration. The Antar dasha is a shorter-term period, lasting several.

3. Pratyantar Dasha: This is a sub-sub-period within an Antar dasha, and is associated with a specific numerical vibration. The Pratyantar Dasha is an even shorter-term period, typically lasting several weeks, during which a person's life is influenced by

the energy associated with the specific numerical vibration.

Maha Dasha

The calculation of Mahadasha involves a few steps:

Step 1: Determine your personality number.

Step 2: Find your ruling planet

Each number is associated with a ruling planet, which determines the Mahadasha cycle. Here are the numbers and their ruling planets:

Number 1: Sun

Number 2: Moon

Number 3: Jupiter

Number 4: Rahu (North Node of the Moon)

Number 5: Mercury

Number 6: Venus

Number 7: Ketu (South Node of the Moon)

Number 8: Saturn

Number 9: Mars

So, if your personality number is 3, your ruling planet is Jupiter, and at birth you are influenced through Jupiter Maha Dasha which lasts for 3 years, during Jupiter Mahadasha person's missing number 3 would help bringing the planet's energy. Next Mahadasha is number 4 and you continue the Mahadasha calculation till Mars lasts for 9 years and subsequently you restart at SUN which is for 1 year long.

20 January 1897:

The person born with the above birth details ruled by the personality number 2 (2+0 = 2) begins with the Moon Mahadasha which lasts for 2 years.

Mahadasha	Starts	Ends
MOON	20 Jan 1897	19 Jan 1899
JUPITER	20 Jan 1899	19 Jan 1902
RAHU	20 Jan 1902	19 Jan 1906
MERCURY	20 Jan 1906	19 Jan 1911
VENUS	20 Jan 1911	19 Jan 1917
KETU	20 Jan 1917	19 Jan 1924
SATURN	20 Jan 1924	19 Jan 1932
MARS	20 Jan 1932	19 Jan 1941
SUN	20 Jan 1941	19 Jan 1942

Antar Dasha

The antardashas are believed to influence different areas of a person's life and be used to gain insights into potential opportunities and challenges during the mahadasha period. For example, if a person is currently in a Jupiter mahadasha period and is experiencing a Venus antardashas, this may indicate a time of increased creativity, romance, or financial growth.

Overall, the antardashas within a mahadasha are an important aspect of Vedic numerology and are used to gain insights into a person's life path and potential during specific periods of time. By understanding the influence of each ruling planet and its associated energies, it is possible to gain a deeper understanding of the mysteries of life and destiny.

Calculating the antardashas within a mahadasha in Vedic numerology involves a specific formula that takes into account the length of the mahadasha and the ruling planet. Here's a step-by-step guide to the calculation:

1. Determine the length of the mahadasha period. MD: MOON (2) 20 Jan 1897 (refer the table previous page)

2. Find the weak-day of birth year details you wish to calculate antar dasha. For 20 Jan 1897 is Wednesday.

3. Get the number for the planet which rules Wednesday, it's the planet Mercury number 5.

4. Now add all the digits exclude the two digits from century 1897 = only 97

2+1+9+7+(week day planet's number)

****2+1+9+7+5 (weekday Wed =5) = 24 = 6**

5. The planet VENUS is number 6, hence from <u>20 Jan 1897 to 19 Jan 1898 this person runs under VENUS (6) antar dasha.</u>

6. Every birthday antar dasha changes based on weekday planet's number, but formula remains same.

Hence, for the for the year <u>1897</u> the person is under MD: MOON (2), and AD: VENUS (6), accordingly predictions are made as we prepare the Vedic grid based on the added MD (Mahadasha), and AD (Antar dasha).

Pratyantar Dasha

The Pratyantar dasha lasts for a shorter-term period, typically lasting several weeks, and is used for:

1. Accurate predictions: Pratyantar Dasha helps us make more accurate predictions about the individual's life. By analysing the effects of each sub-period, we gain a deeper understanding of the individual's life path and the challenges they may face.

2. Personalised analysis: Pratyantar Dasha provides a more personalised analysis of an individual's life which are unique to each person.

3. Insight into future trends: By analysing the Pratyantar dasha, we gain insight into future trends in the individual's life, and this helps the individual prepare for challenges or take advantage of opportunities.

To calculate pratyantar dasha we first calculate both mahadasha , and antradasha, for the same person we have:

MD: MOON (2), AD: VENUS (6)

For the same person the AD: VENUS (6)

from <u>20 Jan 1897 to 19 Jan 1898 and PD: VENUS (6)</u>

***** important to note the PD starts with the same number as AD, in this case PD: 6 for the AD: 6**

<u>PD starts from the same AD this is important</u>

Now, we should multiply the AD and PD to define the number of days pratyantar dasha runs under the planet denotes the same PD, and continue to multiple by changing the PD until it reaches Mars (9) and change back to Sun(1).

Pratyantardasha

20 Jan 1897 - 25 Feb 1897 : (MD: 6 x AD: 6 =36 days)

25 Feb 1897 - 8 Apr 1897: Ketu (MD: 6 x AD: 7 =42 days)

8 Apr 1897 - 5 Jun 1897: Saturn (MD: 6 x AD: 8 = 48 days)

5 Jun 1897 - 29 Jul 1897: Mars (MD: 6 x AD: 9 = 54 days)

As you learn and observed the pratyantar dasha lasts for a few days, weeks within the one year period, once you reach the Mars (9) pratyantar dasha then it starts back to Sun (1) and so on.

Chapter 18

Name Correction

Numerology name correction is a process where an individual's name is altered or modified to align with their other numbers. The aim of name correction is to improve the individual's overall well-being, success, and happiness by aligning their name with the vibrations of their life path number and other important numbers in their numerological chart.

The process of name correction involves analysing the individual's numerological chart to determine their personality number, life path number, name number, and other signifit numbers. The name is then modified or altered by adding or subtracting letters to create a name that resonates more strongly with the individual's numerological chart.

Here are some of the key principles of name correction:

Life path number: The life path number is a key factor in determining the most appropriate name for an individual. The name should be chosen or modified to align with the vibrations of the life path number and to enhance the individual's strengths and overcome their weaknesses.

Name number: The name number is also an important consideration in name correction. The name should be modified to ensure that the name number aligns with the individual's numerological chart and supports their overall well-being and success.

Numerology Chart: Once you have determined the numerical value of your name, you use it to analyse your numerological profile. Each number in Chaldean numerology corresponds to specific energies, traits, and life path characteristics. By understanding your numerological profile, you   gain insights into your personality and life path.

Compatibility: In name correction, the compatibility between an individual's name and their numerological chart is also considered. The name should be modified to ensure that it is compatible with the individual's life path number and other important numbers in their chart.

Culture and tradition: Name correction should be done in a way that respects the individual's culture and traditions. The modified name should be appropriate and meaningful within the individual's cultural context.

Choose a new name: If you decide to change your name based on your numerological profile, you will need to choose a new name that aligns with your desired energies and traits. To do this, you will use the same process to calculate the numerical value of potential new names and choose the one that resonates with you the most.

Legal name change: You need to change it legally. This process vary depending on your location, but it involves filling out a name change application, providing identification documents, and paying a fee.

In conclusion, changing your name based on Chaldean numerology be a powerful tool for gaining insights into your personality and aligning with your true self. However, it is important to approach name changes with care and consideration, as your name is a signifit part of your identity. By following these steps, you make an informed decision and choose a name that supports your personal growth and well-being.

Chapter 19

Numbers and Health

Numerology is a strong instrument for determining a person's personality, life path, and destiny. It , however, be used to get insights on a person's health and well-being. Every number in numerology is related with distinct health issues and treatments that help to alleviate them. In this post, we will look at the relationship between numerology numbers, health problems, and cures.

Number 1:

1 are often ambitious and driven, but they also be prone to stress-related health problems. They are prone to issues with their cardiovascular system, including high blood pressure and heart disease. To remedy these issues, individuals with the number 1 are advised to engage in regular physical activity, nature connection and maintain a healthy diet.

Number 2:

2 tend to be more sensitive and emotional, which make them more susceptible to conditions like anxiety, depression, and digestive issues. They are prone to digestive issues, such as irritable bowel syndrome and acid reflux. To remedy these issues, individuals with the number 2 are advised to consume a diet rich in fiber, avoid processed foods, and practice stress-reducing techniques like meditation and yoga.

Number 3:

3 are often creative and social, but they also be prone to overindulgence in food, alcohol, or drugs. They are prone to respiratory issues, such as asthma and bronchitis. To remedy these issues, individuals with the number 3 are advised to avoid smoking and other irritants, engage in regular exercise, and practice deep breathing exercises.

Number 4:

4 tend to be practical and hardworking, but they also be prone to joint and bone-related issues, like arthritis and osteoporosis. They are prone to issues with their musculoskeletal system, including arthritis and joint pain. To remedy these issues, individuals with the number 4 are

advised to engage in regular exercise, maintain a healthy weight, and practice stress-reducing techniques like massage and yoga.

Number 5:

5 tend to be adventurous and independent, but they also be prone to accidents and injuries. They are prone to issues with their nervous system, including anxiety and depression. To remedy these issues, individuals with the number 5 are advised to engage in regular exercise, practice stress-reducing techniques like meditation and yoga, and consume a diet rich in omega-3 fatty acids.

Number 6:

6 tend to be nurturing and caring, but they also be prone to stress-related conditions like anxiety and insomnia. They are prone to issues with their reproductive system, including fertility issues and menstrual problems. to remedy these issues, individuals with the number 6 are advised to maintain a healthy weight, consume a diet rich in vitamins and minerals, and engage in regular exercise.

Number 7:

7 tend to be introspective and spiritual, but they also be prone to digestive issues and skin-related problems. They are prone to issues with their immune system, including allergies and autoimmune diseases. To remedy these issues, individuals with the number 7 are advised to consume a diet rich in antioxidants, engage in regular exercise, and practice stress-reducing techniques like meditation and yoga.

Number 8:

8 tend to be ambitious and successful, but they also be prone to stress-related conditions like high blood pressure and heart disease. They are prone to issues with their digestive system, including constipation and indigestion. To remedy these issues, individuals with the number 8 are advised to consume a diet rich in fiber, avoid processed foods, and engage in regular exercise.

Number 9:

9 tend to be compassionate and intuitive, but they also be prone to immune-related disorders like allergies and autoimmune diseases.. They are prone to issues with their circulatory system, including varicose veins and poor

circulation. To remedy these issues, individuals with the number 9 are advised to engage in regular exercise, maintain a healthy weight, and consume a diet rich in vitamins and minerals. Numerology offers a unique perspective on health, diseases, and remedies. it is possible to identify potential health risks and take steps to prevent or treat them.

Chapter 20

Conclusion

In this book, we have examined the domain of numerology and its numerous applications in our lives. We have seen how each number has its unique vibrational energy and how these energies might provide insight into ourselves and our surroundings.

You construct an individual numerology chart by figuring out the numbers in our name and birthdate, which reveal essential understandings of our character, talents, shortcomings, and journey. We use this knowledge to make better judgements, live more consciously, and achieve our objectives.

Numerology give us a view of our interactions with others. Analysing the numerical patterns and energies between two people, we acquire a better knowledge of the dynamics of our relationships and illustrate potential regions for growth and advancement.

You use numerology as a tool for understanding our physical, emotional, and spiritual health. By examining the numerical patterns and tendencies in our lives, we find potential health risks and take preventative measures to support our well-being.

Numerology offer insight into our future and help us navigate the challenges and opportunities that lie ahead. By examining the numerical patterns and energies of the current year and month, we   gain insight into the energies and influences that will shape our experiences and decisions.

Overall, the knowledge and wisdom of numerology have a profound impact on our lives, and we encourage you to continue exploring this fascinating field. If you are seeking guidance in your personal or professional life, numerology be a valuable tool for self-discovery and growth.

As we close this book, we hope it has served as a comprehensive guide to the world of numerology and that you have gained valuable insights and knowledge that you apply to your life. We encourage you to continue exploring the limitless potential of numerology and to use its principles to create a life of purpose, fulfilment, and joy.

About the author

Santu Roy is a computer programmer turned author with a passion for self-care and spirituality. Born and raised in Assam, India, Santu developed an early interest in programming and pursued a degree in Computer Science. After graduation, he worked for several years in the tech industry, honing his skills and gaining valuable experience.

However, Santu's interest in self-care and spirituality continued to grow, and he eventually decided to pursue his passion for writing. In 2018, he published his first book, "The Power of Self Brainwash" which was well-received by readers and critics alike.

Inspired by his spiritual interests in numerology and astrology, Santu began exploring the concept of destiny and its role in our lives. After years of research and introspection, he has recently published his latest work, "Unlocking Your Destiny."

In this book, Santu shares his insights on how we tap into our true potential and fulfil our destiny. Through a combination of numerology, astrology, and personal anecdotes, he offers practical advice and guidance on how to overcome obstacles, find our purpose, and create the life we truly want.

Santu continues to be an active member of the spiritual community and regularly participates in workshops and events focused on self-care and personal development. When he's not writing or programming, he enjoys spending time with his family and cooking new dishes.